Essential Forms For Self Advocacy

NAVIGATING

PUBLIC

SCHOOL

A Guide To Education Law

A Kelly Neal, Esq.
Neal Student Support Advocacy & Disability, LLC

Library of Congress Control Number: 2025911415

ISBN No: 979-8-9929441-3-6

Cover design by A. Kelly Neal, Esq.

Printed in the United States of America

For more information, visit www.SSAdisability.org

Disclaimer:

This book is a battle cry. A call to expose the failures, the indifference, and the willful neglect that have stolen futures and shattered spirits. It is dedicated to every educator who has looked away instead of stepping up, who has denied services for convenience, who has hidden behind bureaucracy instead of doing what is right. You know exactly who you are. Your inaction has forced parents into exhausting, merciless fights for the bare minimum—the rights their children are both legally and morally owed.

To the parents who have been dismissed, manipulated, and told to 'trust the process' while watching their child suffer—this book is your weapon. Use it to tear through the excuses, to shine a glaring light on the system's failures, to demand what should never have been denied. Because if they refuse to fight for your child, you will. And you will win.

Power to Our Pupils.

To everyone who contributed to this book, thank you from the bottom of my heart. Your support, insights, and efforts have been invaluable, and I am deeply grateful. Your contributions have not gone unnoticed—they have made this book possible, and I appreciate each and every one of you.

TABLE OF CONTENTS

For far too long, parents have been forced to navigate a system that pretends to serve children with disabilities while drowning them in bureaucracy, delays, and outright denial. I have seen it firsthand—the way schools manipulate the process, the way educators, whether out of ignorance or apathy, refuse to provide the support children so desperately need, and the way parents are left feeling helpless, exhausted, and alone in a battle they never should have to fight.

I wrote this book because enough is enough.

This is more than a guide; it is a weapon for change. It arms parents, advocates, and the educators who truly care with the knowledge they need to cut through the lies, the confusion, and the systemic failures that keep children from receiving the education they deserve. The IDEA eligibility process should not be a battle of wills. Parents should not have to become legal experts just to secure what the law already guarantees. And yet—here we are.

Let this book be both your shield and your sword—a shield to protect against the system's relentless obstacles, and a sword to slash through the excuses, the gaslighting, and the negligence that stand between children and their rightful education.

If you are a parent reading this, know this: You are not alone. You are not imagining things. You are not asking for too much. Your child has rights, and those rights are non-negotiable.

And to those within the system who continue to fail these children—consider this your warning. Parents are waking up. Parents are fighting. And parents will win.

—A. Kelly Neal, Esq.

These documents are the result of years of fighting for students and families in the education system. They have been invaluable in my practice, and now, they are in your hands—to use, to demand change, and to ensure that no child is left behind due to neglect or bureaucracy.

Now is the time to act. Use these tools to hold schools accountable, to challenge the injustices, and to break down the barriers that keep children from the education they deserve. Together, we can dismantle the school-to-prison pipeline and build a system that truly serves all students.

Stand up. Speak out. Fight back. Our children are counting on us.

ADDENDUM TO THE STUDENT CODE OF CONDUCT

All disciplinary actions involving my child/student, who is identified as having a disability, must comply with the requirements of Section 504 of the Rehabilitation Act of 1973, the Individuals with Disabilities Education Act (IDEA), the Americans with Disabilities Act (ADA) and the State's Special Education Rules. Accordingly, the consequences for any unwanted behaviors shall be individualized to address my child/student's unique needs and shall take precedence over the standard consequences outlined in the school's Code of Conduct. Failure to adhere to these requirements will result in the filing of an ethics complaint against the teaching credentials of the violator.

_____

Parent/Guardian Signature   Date

Although Gebser originally dealt with teacher-on-student sexual harassment, courts have extended the notice + deliberate indifference standard to peer-to-peer harassment, including:
- Sex-based bullying (Title IX),
- Disability-based harassment (Section 504 / ADA),
- Sometimes race-based harassment (under Title VI).

To Establish Liability:

The victim must show that the school:
1. Had actual knowledge of the bullying/harassment, and
2. An appropriate person with authority to take corrective measures received that knowledge, and
3. The school acted with deliberate indifference, meaning:
   o It responded in a way that was clearly unreasonable,
   o Or did nothing when action was clearly necessary.

Severe, Pervasive, and Objectively Offensive"

The harassment must be:
- Severe (not just name-calling),
- Pervasive (recurring or widespread),
- Objectively offensive (would affect any reasonable student),
- And must interfere with the victim's access to education.

So: one isolated comment usually isn't enough for liability under Gebser—but ongoing, documented bullying that affects attendance or performance could be.

How Schools Receive "Gebser Notice" of Bullying:

Here are common ways schools get actual notice:
- A parent complains in writing or at a meeting.
- A teacher, counselor, or administrator observes the bullying or is told by the student.
- A student tells a staff member who has the authority (e.g., principal, assistant principal).
- There's a discipline referral documenting the conduct.

Once that happens, if the school doesn't investigate or intervene appropriately, they risk liability.

How Gebser Notice is Used in These Cases:
- Plaintiffs cite it to show the school failed in its legal duty.
- Defendants (schools) try to prove they didn't have actual knowledge or that their response wasn't deliberately indifferent.
- Courts analyze timing, documentation, and the school's response

STATE OF_____
COUNTY OF_____

Parent Name]	
Parent Address]	
City/State/Zip]	
Parent/Legal Guardian]	STUDENT NAME
To]	STUDENT DOB
School Principal]	
School Name]	
School Address]	
School City/State/Zip]	
Respondent]	

GEBSER NOTICE OF SEVERE AND PERVASIVE BULLYING

I am writing to formally notify [School Name] of ongoing, severe, and pervasive harassment that my child, [Student's Full Name], a [Grade Level] student at your school, has been subjected to by other students. This harassment has included the following behaviors:

- [Brief description, e.g., "Verbal name-calling using slurs related to their disability/gender/ethnicity"]
- [Physical bullying, e.g., "Shoved in the hallway on multiple occasions"]
- [Cyberbullying, e.g., "Group chats and social media posts targeting my child"]

These incidents have occurred on multiple occasions since [start date], including but not limited to [list a few dates or specific incidents]. I have attached supporting documentation, including prior emails, screenshots, and any reports made to teachers or staff.

This harassment is interfering with my child's ability to access their education and is causing significant emotional distress. [He/She/They] have expressed fear about attending school and have experienced a noticeable decline in academic performance and well-being.

I am providing this notice to you as someone in a position of authority to take corrective action. Under Title IX, Section 504, and ADA, the school has a legal obligation to promptly investigate and remedy harassment that denies a student equal access to education.

I request the following:
1. An immediate investigation into the reported harassment.
2. Appropriate measures to ensure my child's safety at school.
3. Information about any findings and steps the school plans to take.
4. A copy of the school's anti-bullying, Title IX, and Section 504 grievance procedures.

NAME OF SCHOOL DISTRICT receives federal funds for which it contracts to not discriminate. You have the authority to investigate and correct this discrimination. You have control over the site and personnel where the discrimination occurs. If you do not investigate and correct the problem, we may claim that you and the district are deliberately indifferent to the discrimination. If you do not correct unlawful discrimination, you may be liable personally for damages, and the school district may also be liable for damages.

Please confirm receipt of this letter and let me know what steps will be taken. I appreciate your prompt attention to this matter and your commitment to ensuring a safe learning environment for all students. I look forward to receiving a response and the results of any investigation within 10 days of the date of this notice.

_____

Parent/Legal Guardian of Above Named Student   Date

Cc: superintendent
        all board members
        special education director
        (names of anyone else to be held legally liable).

FORMAL COMPLAINTS

A special education formal complaint is a written complaint filed with a state education agency (SEA) when a parent, guardian, or other party believes that a school district has violated the Individuals with Disabilities Education Act (IDEA). This process is different from a due process complaint, which leads to a hearing. Instead, a formal complaint triggers an investigation by the SEA.

Key Aspects of a Formal Complaint

1. Who Can File?
   o Parents or guardians of a student with disabilities
   o Advocacy organizations
   o Other individuals or groups aware of violations
2. What Can It Address?
   o Failure to provide Free Appropriate Public Education (FAPE)
   o Failure to follow an Individualized Education Program (IEP)
   o Violations related to Child Find obligations
   o Procedural violations under IDEA
   o Systemic violations affecting multiple students
3. Where to File?
   o The complaint is submitted to the state education agency (SEA) in the state where the alleged violation occurred.
4. Timeline for Filing
   o The violation must have occurred within one year before the complaint is filed.
5. Investigation Process
   o The SEA reviews the complaint and may ask for additional information.
   o The school district is given an opportunity to respond and may propose a resolution.
   o The SEA conducts an investigation, which may include document reviews and interviews.
   o The SEA must issue a written decision within 60 calendar days, unless an extension is granted.
6. Possible Outcomes
   o The SEA may find the school compliant or noncompliant with IDEA.
   o If noncompliant, the SEA may require corrective actions, such as:
     ▪ Training for school staff
     ▪ Compensatory education services for the student
     ▪ Policy changes

Why File a Formal Complaint?
- It's a good option for systemic violations or when seeking policy changes.
- It doesn't require a lawyer or formal hearing process.
- It can lead to faster resolutions compared to due process hearings.

For more information on filing a formal complaint visit the website: https://gadoe.org/federal-programs/filing-formal-complaints-under-essa/

For more information on your state's formal complaint process contact your state's educational authority. A complete list of websites is in the appendix.

DUE PROCESS

Special education due process refers to the legal procedures and protections that ensure students with disabilities receive a free appropriate public education (FAPE) as required by the Individuals with Disabilities Education Act (IDEA). These procedures are designed to resolve disagreements between parents and school districts about the identification, evaluation, placement, and provision of services for a student with disabilities.

Here's an overview of special education due process:

1. Notice of Procedural Safeguards
Schools must provide parents with a "Notice of Procedural Safeguards" outlining their rights under IDEA. This includes the right to participate in meetings, access to educational records, and the right to resolve disputes through due process.

2. Dispute Resolution Options
If parents and the school district disagree about any aspect of the student's education, IDEA provides several mechanisms to resolve the conflict:
- Mediation: A voluntary, non-adversarial process in which a neutral third party helps the parties reach an agreement.
- Due Process Hearing: A formal, legal proceeding where both parties present their case before an impartial hearing officer. This process may involve the submission of evidence, witness testimony, and legal arguments.
- State Complaint Procedures: A formal process where parents can file a complaint with the state education agency if they believe that a school district has violated IDEA.

3. Due Process Hearing
If a dispute is not resolved through mediation, a parent or school district may request a due process hearing. The hearing officer listens to both sides, reviews evidence, and makes a legally binding decision. The hearing process includes:
- Filing a Complaint: The parent or school files a written complaint outlining the specific disagreement, such as issues with evaluation, placement, or services.
- Resolution Session: A meeting between the parents and school officials to try to resolve the issues before going to a hearing.
- Hearing: The formal due process hearing where each side presents their case.
- Decision: After the hearing, the officer issues a written decision that resolves the dispute.

4. Stay-Put Provision
During a due process hearing, the "stay-put" provision ensures that the student remains in their current educational placement until the dispute is resolved, unless the parents and the school agree to a change.

5. Appeal Process

If either party disagrees with the decision from the due process hearing, they can appeal to the state or federal court.

6. Timelines

There are strict timelines for each step of the due process, including filing complaints, scheduling hearings, and issuing decisions. These timelines are intended to ensure the process moves forward efficiently.

Key Areas of Dispute in Special Education Due Process:
- Eligibility: Whether the student qualifies for special education services.
- Free Appropriate Public Education (FAPE): Whether the school is providing services in accordance with the student's Individualized Education Program (IEP).
- Evaluation: Disagreements about the adequacy or type of evaluations conducted.
- Placement: Disputes about where and how the student should be educated.
- Services: Disagreements about the specific services the student needs or is receiving.

Special education due process is a crucial safeguard that ensures that students with disabilities have their educational rights protected and that parents have a mechanism to address concerns and disagreements with school districts.

In GA you can find the form to request due process here: https://gadoe.org/special-education/due-process-hearings-and-decisions/

To find out how to file a due process request in your state contact your state educational authority. A list of all 50 websites are in the appendix of this book.

COMPLAINTS AGAINST EDUCATORS

Complaints against educators generally involve allegations of misconduct, incompetence, or violations of professional standards. These complaints can be filed by students, parents, colleagues, administrators, or the general public. The process varies by state and school district, but here's an overview of how complaints are typically handled:

1. Grounds for Complaints

Complaints against educators can be based on various concerns, including:

- Professional Misconduct – Inappropriate behavior, including harassment, discrimination, or improper relationships with students.
- Ethical Violations – Breaches of professional conduct, such as dishonesty, falsifying records, or misuse of school funds.
- Incompetence – Repeated failure to meet teaching standards or an inability to effectively educate students.
- Neglect of Duty – Failing to fulfill responsibilities, including poor classroom management, excessive absenteeism, or refusal to follow school policies.
- Criminal Activity – Criminal offenses, including drug use, theft, assault, or endangerment of students.
- License or Certification Issues – Teaching without proper credentials or falsifying qualifications.

2. Who Can File a Complaint?

- Students or parents
- Fellow educators or school staff
- School administrators
- State licensing agencies
- Law enforcement

3. How the Complaint Process Works

The process varies by state and school district, but typically follows these steps:

Step 1: Filing the Complaint

- Complaints are usually submitted in writing to the school district, state education department, or professional licensing board.
- The complaint must include specific details, evidence, and supporting documentation.

Step 2: Initial Review

- The school or licensing agency determines if the complaint has merit.
- Minor issues may be handled at the school level through informal mediation or corrective action.

Step 3: Investigation

- If the complaint is serious, an investigation is conducted, which may include:
    - Interviews with witnesses, students, and the accused educator
    - Review of classroom materials, emails, or other records
    - Possible involvement of law enforcement (if criminal activity is alleged)

Step 4: Disciplinary Action
- If the complaint is substantiated, disciplinary actions may include:
    - Warnings or reprimands – A formal note in the educator's file
    - Suspension – Temporary removal from duties
    - License revocation – Loss of teaching credentials
    - Termination – Dismissal from employment
    - Legal consequences – Criminal charges if laws were violated

Step 5: Appeals Process
- Educators have the right to appeal disciplinary actions, which may involve a hearing before a state board or administrative judge.

4. Reporting to State Licensing Boards

In cases involving serious misconduct, the complaint may be reported to the state's educator licensing board, which can take additional action, including suspending or revoking teaching credentials.

5. Confidentiality and Public Records
- Some complaints and investigations remain confidential, while others (especially serious disciplinary actions) may become part of the public record.
- Many states maintain a database where the public can check if an educator has faced disciplinary action.

To file complaints against educators in Georgia you can get the forms and rules from the Georgia Professional Standards Commission and here is there website: www.gapsc.com

To find the eductor complaint process in your state, a list of the educator credentialing entities for all 50 states with their websites is in the appendix of this book.

Georgia Professional Standards Commission
General Complaint Form for Public Submission

Date of Complaint* _____

Educator's Full Name* _____

Educator's Address _____

Educator's Work Phone _____

Educator's School System or Agency* _____

Educator's School or Program* _____

Educator's Employment Position* _____

Briefly describe the alleged violation of Code of Ethics for Educators or the reason for your complaint. Include dates and time of alleged violations.*

Attach a list of witnesses and other persons who have knowledge of the facts alleged in the complaint. Include names, addresses and telephone numbers if known. Attach pertinent documentation or evidence.

Complainant - Name of Person(s) Filing the Complaint*_____

Complainant's Signature* _____

Complainant's Address* _____

_____

Complainant's Phone Number* _____

Complainant's Email Address _____

***Information Required - An unsigned complaint cannot be processed.**

Mail to: Educator Ethics, 200 Piedmont Avenue, Suite 1716, Atlanta, GA 30334-9032
OR
Email to: Ethics@GaPSC.com

Contact Numbers: (404) 232-2700 or (800) 537-5996 FAX (404) 232-2720

EDUCATION DISCRIMINATION & CIVIL RIGHTS COMPLAINTS

Education discrimination occurs when students are treated unfairly based on protected characteristics such as race, gender, disability, national origin, or religion. Civil rights complaints in education typically involve violations of federal laws designed to ensure equal access to education. These complaints are often investigated by the U.S. Department of Education's Office for Civil Rights (OCR) or other relevant agencies.

1. What Is Education Discrimination?
Education discrimination occurs when students face unequal treatment in schools, colleges, or other educational institutions. It can take various forms, including:

A. Types of Discrimination
1. Disability Discrimination (Violates Section 504 of the Rehabilitation Act & ADA)
   o Denying accommodations to students with disabilities
   o Unlawful exclusion from programs or activities
   o Failure to provide necessary special education services (IDEA violations)
2. Race, Color, or National Origin Discrimination (Violates Title VI of the Civil Rights Act)
   o Unequal disciplinary actions targeting certain racial groups
   o Segregation or racial bias in admissions and school policies
   o Harassment or bullying based on race or national origin
3. Sex or Gender Discrimination (Violates Title IX of the Education Amendments)
   o Unequal access to sports, scholarships, or academic programs
   o Sexual harassment, including teacher or peer misconduct
   o Discrimination against pregnant or parenting students
4. Religious Discrimination
   o Denying students the right to express religious beliefs
   o Unequal treatment based on religious dress or practices
5. LGBTQ+ Discrimination
   o Harassment based on gender identity or sexual orientation
   o Unequal access to facilities or participation in school activities

2. Where to File Civil Rights Complaints in Education
A. U.S. Department of Education – Office for Civil Rights (OCR)
Website: https://www2.ed.gov/about/offices/list/ocr/complaintintro.html
- Investigates complaints against schools, districts, and colleges that receive federal funding
- Covers issues related to race, sex, disability, and national origin discrimination

B. U.S. Department of Justice – Civil Rights Division
Website: https://www.justice.gov/crt   Complaint form: https://civilrights.justice.gov/report/
- Handles cases involving systemic discrimination in public schools

C. State Education Agencies
- Many states have their own civil rights offices or human rights commissions

D. Local School Districts
- Schools often have their own procedures for handling discrimination complaints

3. How to File a Civil Rights Complaint
Step 1: Identify the Violation
- Determine if the issue involves discrimination under federal law.
- Collect evidence, such as emails, school policies, or witness statements.

Step 2: Submit the Complaint
- File with OCR online, by mail, or via email.
- Complaints must generally be filed within 180 days of the discriminatory act.

Step 3: Investigation Process
- The agency reviews the complaint and may launch an investigation.
- Investigators may conduct interviews, review policies, and examine records.

Step 4: Resolution & Enforcement
- Schools may be required to change policies, provide training, or compensate victims.
- If violations are found and not corrected, federal funding may be withheld.

4. Example Cases of Education Discrimination
- A school suspends Black students at a significantly higher rate than White students for the same behavior.
- A deaf student is denied a sign language interpreter in class.
- A pregnant student is forced to withdraw from extracurricular activities.
- A transgender student is denied access to bathrooms that align with their gender identity

To find out whether your state educational authority has their own civil rights offices or human rights commissions you can contact them. All 50 state's websites are in the appendix of this book.

The US Department of Justice Complaint form is here: https://www.ada.gov/assets/pdfs/file-a-complaint-lg.pdf? In my experience The US Department of Justice-Office of Civil Rights is far better at handling complaints than the US Department of Education, although that's an option.

U.S. Department of Justice

Civil Rights Division

Federal Coordination and Compliance Section - NWB
950 Pennsylvania Ave, NW
Washington, DC 20530

COMPLAINT FORM

The purpose of this form is to assist you in filing a complaint with the Federal Coordination and Compliance Section. You are not required to use this form; a letter with the same information is sufficient. However, the information requested in the items marked with a star (*) must be provided, whether or not this form is used.

1.* State your name and address.

Name: _____

Address: _____

_____ Zip _____

Telephone: Home: (_____)_____ Work or Cell: (_____)_____

2.* Person(s) discriminated against, if different from above:

Name: _____

Address: _____

_____ Zip _____

Telephone: Home: (_____)_____ Work or Cell: (_____)_____
Please explain your relationship to this person(s).

3.* Agency and department or program that discriminated:

Name: _____

Address: _____

_____ Zip _____

Telephone: Home: (_____)_____ Work or Cell: (_____)_____

4A.* Non-employment: Does your complaint concern discrimination in the delivery of services or in other discriminatory actions of the department or agency in its treatment of you or others? If so, please indicate below the base(s) on which you believe these discriminatory actions were taken.

_____ Race/Ethnicity: _____

_____ National origin: _____

_____ Sex: _____

_____ Religion: _____

_____ Age: _____

_____ Disability: _____

4B.* Employment: Does your complaint concern discrimination in employment by the department or agency? If so, please indicate below the base(s) on which you believe these discriminatory actions were taken.

_____ Race/Ethnicity: _____

_____ National origin: _____

_____ Sex: _____

_____ Religion: _____

_____ Age: _____

_____ Disability: _____

5. What is the most convenient time and place for us to contact you about this complaint?

_____

6. If we will not be able to reach you directly, you may wish to give us the name and phone number of a person who can tell us how to reach you and/or provide information about your complaint:

Name:

_____

Telephone: Home:(_____)_____ Work or Cell: (_____)_____

7. If you have an attorney representing you concerning the matters raised in this complaint, please provide the following:

Name: _____

Address: _____

_____ Zip_____

Telephone: Home: (_____)_____Work or Cell: (_____)_____

8.* To your best recollection, on what date(s) did the alleged discrimination take place?

Earliest date of discrimination:

_____

Most recent date of discrimination:

_____

9. Complaints of discrimination must generally be filed within 180 days of the alleged discrimination. If the most recent date of discrimination, listed above, is more than 180 days ago, you may request a waiver of the filing requirement. If you wish to request a waiver, please explain why you waited until now to file your complaint.

_____

_____

_____

10.* Please explain as clearly as possible what happened, why you believe it happened, and how you were discriminated against. Indicate who was involved. Be sure to include how other persons were treated differently from you. (Please use additional sheets if necessary and attach a copy of written materials pertaining to your case.)

_____

_____

_____

_____

_____

_____

_____

_____

_____

_____

_____

_____

_____

_____

_____

_____

_____

11. The laws we enforce prohibit recipients of Department of Justice funds from intimidating or retaliating against anyone because he or she has either taken action or participated in action to secure rights protected by these laws. If you believe that you have been retaliated against (separate from the discrimination alleged in #10), please explain the circumstances below. Be sure to explain what actions you took which you believe were the basis for the alleged retaliation.

_____

_____

_____

_____

_____

_____

_____

_____

_____

12. Please list below any persons (witnesses, fellow employees, supervisors, or others), if known, whom we may contact for additional information to support or clarify your complaint.

Name: _____

Address: _____

_____ Zip_____

Telephone: Home: (_____)_____Work or Cell: (_____)_____

_____

_____

_____

_____

_____

_____

13. Do you have any other information that you think is relevant to our investigation of your allegations?

_____

_____

_____

_____

_____

_____

_____

_____

_____

_____

14. What remedy are you seeking for the alleged discrimination?

_____

_____

_____

15. Have you (or the person discriminated against) filed the same or any other complaints with other offices of the Department of Justice (including the Office of Justice Programs, Federal Bureau of Investigation, etc.)?

Yes _____ No _____

If so, do you remember the Complaint Number?

_____

Against what agency and department or program was it filed?

_____

Address: _____

_____ Zip _____

Telephone No: (____)_____ Date of Filing: _____

DOJ Agency:_____ Briefly, what was the complaint about?

_____

_____

_____

What was the result?

_____

_____

_____

16.   Have you filed or do you intend to file a charge or complaint concerning the matters raised in this complaint with any of the following?

_____ U.S. Equal Employment Opportunity Commission

_____ Federal or State Court

_____ Your State or local Human Relations/Rights Commission

_____ Grievance or complaint office

17.   If you have already filed a charge or complaint with an agency indicated in #16, above, please provide the following information (attach additional pages if necessary):

Agency: _____

Date filed: _____

Case or Docket Number: _____

Date of Trial/Hearing: _____

Location of Agency/Court: _____

Name of Investigator: _____

Status of Case: _____

Comments: _____

_____

_____

_____

18. While it is not necessary for you to know about aid that the agency or institution you are filing against receives from the Federal government, if you know of any Department of Justice funds or assistance received by the program or department in which the alleged discrimination occurred, please provide that information below.

_____

_____

_____

19.* We cannot accept a complaint if it has not been signed. Please sign and date this Complaint Form below.

_____   _____

(Signature)   (Date)

Please feel free to add additional sheets to explain the present situation to us.

We will need your consent to disclose your name, if necessary, in the course of any investigation. Therefore, we will need a signed Consent Form from you. (If you are filing this complaint for a person whom you allege has been discriminated against, we will in most instances need a signed Consent Form from that person.) See the "Notice about Investigatory Uses of Personal Information" for information about the Consent Form. Please mail the completed, signed Discrimination Complaint Form and the signed Consent Form (please make one copy of each for your records) to:

United States Department of Justice
Civil Rights Division
Federal Coordination and Compliance Section - NWB
950 Pennsylvania Avenue, NW
Washington, D.C. 20530

Toll-free Voice and TDD: (888) 848-5306
Voice: (202) 307-2222
TDD: (202) 307-2678

20. How did you learn that you could file this complaint?

_____

_____

_____

21. If your complaint has already been assigned a DOJ complaint number, please list it here:

_____

Note: If a currently valid OMB control number is not displayed on the first page, you are not required to fill out this complaint form unless the Department of Justice has begun an administrative investigation into this complaint.

FAMILY EDUCATIONAL RIGHTS & PRIVACY ACT(FERPA) COMPLAINTS

A FERPA complaint is a formal written allegation that a school, district, or education agency violated a student's privacy rights under FERPA. These rights include:

- The right to access the student's education records.
- The right to request that inaccurate records be amended.
- The right to control disclosure of personally identifiable information (PII) from those records.

Who Can File a Complaint?

- A parent or eligible student (18+ or in postsecondary education).
- The complaint must be filed within 180 days of the alleged violation.

How to File a FERPA Complaint
Complaints must be in writing and sent to the Student Privacy Policy Office (SPPO) at the U.S. Department of Education.
Contact Info:
Student Privacy Policy Office
U.S. Department of Education
400 Maryland Ave, SW
Washington, DC 20202-8520
https://studentprivacy.ed.gov
The complaint should include:

- The name and contact info of the complainant
- Details about the school or agency involved
- A description of the alleged FERPA violation
- Relevant dates and facts

What Happens After a Complaint is Filed?

1. Acknowledgement: SPPO confirms receipt.
2. Review: They assess whether the complaint meets the requirements.
3. Investigation (if accepted):
   o They may contact the school and request information.
   o Both parties can provide evidence.
4. Resolution:
   o If a violation is found, SPPO will work with the school to correct it.
   o FERPA does not allow for damages or private lawsuits — the remedy is typically correction of the violation and compliance going forward.

Common Reasons for FERPA Complaints

- Denial of access to student records
- Improper release of records without consent
- Failure to amend inaccurate or misleading records
- Releasing data without following FERPA's disclosure rules

STATE OF _____

COUNTY OF_____

Parent/Student Name	]
Parent/Student Address	]
P/S, City/State/Zip	]
Parent/Legal Guardian	]
	] STUDENT NAME
To	] STUDENT DOB
Student Privacy Policy Office	]
U.S. Department of Education	]
400 Maryland Avenue, SW	]
Washington, DC 20202-8520	]
FERPA.Complaints@ed.gov	]
Respondent	]

FAMILY EDUCATIONAL RIGHTS & PRIVACY ACT (FERPA) COMPLAINT

I am writing to file a formal complaint under the Family Educational Rights and Privacy Act (FERPA), 20 U.S.C. § 1232g, and its implementing regulations, 34 C.F.R. Part 99.

I believe that [Name of School or Agency] has violated my [or my child's] rights under FERPA as follows:

Description of Violation:
[Clearly describe what happened, including dates, details of the incident, and why you believe it violates FERPA. Include whether access to records was denied, personally identifiable information was improperly disclosed, or records were not properly amended.]

Date of the Violation:
[Insert the date(s)]

I respectfully request that the Department investigate this matter and take appropriate corrective action.

Thank you for your attention to this matter.

_____   _____
Parent/Guardian Signature   Date

School evaluations are critically important for identifying and supporting students' unique learning needs. Here's why they matter:

1. Early Identification of Needs

Evaluations help detect learning disabilities, developmental delays, emotional challenges, or behavioral issues early. The sooner a student's needs are identified, the sooner they can get support—and early intervention is often more effective.

2. Eligibility for Special Education Services

Under the Individuals with Disabilities Education Act (IDEA), a formal evaluation is the first step in determining whether a child qualifies for special education services. Without it, a student may not receive the support they are legally entitled to.

3. Customized Educational Planning

Evaluations provide a detailed understanding of a student's strengths and challenges. This information is essential for creating an Individualized Education Program (IEP) or Section 504 Plan, which are tailored to meet the student's specific needs.

4. Ensures Educational Equity

By identifying students who need additional support, evaluations promote educational equity. They help close achievement gaps for students with disabilities, those from marginalized communities, and those facing other barriers to learning.

5. Informs Teaching Strategies

Results from evaluations guide educators in choosing the most effective teaching methods and classroom accommodations, leading to better academic outcomes and a more inclusive classroom environment.

6. Supports Behavior and Mental Health

Evaluations can uncover emotional or behavioral disorders, such as ADHD or anxiety, that may be impacting a student's performance. With this knowledge, schools can provide behavioral supports or counseling services.

STATE OF _____
COUNTY OF _____

Parent/Student Name	]
Parent/Student Address	]
P/S, City/State/Zip	]
Parent/Legal Guardian	]
	] STUDENT NAME
To	] STUDENT DOB
School Name	]
School Address	]
School City/State/Zip	]
Respondent	]

CONSENT AND REQUEST FOR EVALUATION

This document serves as consent to evaluate the above named student in accordance with 34 CFR 300.304(c)(4) that requires evaluation in all areas of suspected disability including, but not limited to, health, vision, hearing, social and emotional status, general intelligence, academic performance, communicative status, and motor abilities. The following specific evaluations are requested:

HEARING/VISION
SOCIAL/EMOTIONAL
ACHIEVEMENT/INTELLIGENCE COMPREHENSIVE PSYCHO-EDUCATIONAL EVAL
SPEECH/LANGUAGE EVALUATION BY A SPEECH LANGUAGE PATHOLOGIST
COMMUNICATION EVALUATION WITH ALL SEVEN C'S
FUNCTIONAL BEHAVIORAL ASSESSMENT BY A BOARD CERTIFIED BEHAVIORAL ANALYST
MOTOR/OCCUPATIONAL THERPAY EVALUATION
ASSISTIVE DEVICE EVALUATION
WRAP AROUND SERVICES AND RESIDENTIAL PLACEMENT EVALUATION
VOCATIONAL REHABILITATION/TRAINING

Request for the above referenced evaluations are made in accordance with 34 CFR 300.301 and 300.303. Therefore, initial evaluations are expected to be completed with sixty (60) days from the date of consent below. Re-evaluations are expected to be completed in a reasonable amount of time but no later than three years from the date of the initial evaluation in accordance with 34 CFR 300.303(b)(2)

_____   _____
Parent/Legal Guardian of Above Named Student   Date of Consent

Student constitutional rights refer to the legal protections students have under the U.S. Constitution, even while they are in school. While students do not shed their constitutional rights at the schoolhouse gate, those rights can be balanced against the school's need to maintain a safe and orderly environment. Here's a breakdown of the most important rights:

First Amendment – Freedom of Speech and Expression
- Students have the right to express themselves, including wearing armbands, clothing with messages, or speaking out—so long as it doesn't cause substantial disruption to the learning environment (per *Tinker v. Des Moines*, 1969).
- Schools can limit speech that is vulgar, promotes illegal drug use (*Morse v. Frederick*), or is part of a school-sponsored activity (*Hazelwood v. Kuhlmeier*).

Fourth Amendment – Protection Against Unreasonable Searches and Seizures
- Students have a right to privacy, but it is limited in school.
- School officials can search a student or their belongings (like backpacks or lockers) if they have "reasonable suspicion" that a rule or law has been broken (*New Jersey v. T.L.O.*, 1985).
- Random drug testing of student-athletes and others in extracurriculars has been upheld as constitutional.

Fourteenth Amendment – Due Process and Equal Protection
- Due Process: Students must be given fair procedures when facing serious disciplinary actions, like suspension or expulsion. This includes notice of the charges and an opportunity to be heard.
- Equal Protection: Schools cannot discriminate based on race, sex, disability, or other protected statuses. This applies to school discipline, access to programs, and general treatment.

Right to Education (State Constitutions)
- While the U.S. Constitution does not guarantee the right to education, state constitutions do, and federal protections (like IDEA, Title IX, and Section 504) ensure access and fairness in education.

STATE OF _____
COUNTY OF _____

PARENT NAME   ]
Parent address   ]
Parent City/State/Zip   ]
Phone #   ]
Email Address   ]
                                               ]
                                               ]   STUDENT NAME
                    To   ]   Date of Birth 00/00/0000
SCHOOL SYSTEM   ]
School Address   ]
School City/State/Zip   ]
Phone # / Fax #   ]
Email Address   ]
                                               ]

CONSTITUTIONAL RIGHTS NOTICE

As a citizen of the United States of America, and under my Constitutional Rights, if you wish to question, detain, or otherwise assess me in regard to any disciplinary manner, I have the right to remain silent, you will call/contact my parent(s)/guardian(s) at the numbers/email address made available below. Because I am a minor, my rights remain in effect until waived in writing by all parties below. While we understand the school is the in loco parentis with the authority to question a student, it is NOT insubordination to delay questioning until a parent/guardian is present.

_____   _____
STUDENT SIGNATURE   Date

Parent Phone Numbers/E-mail address:

_____   _____
Father/(add name in print/sign above)   Date

_____   _____
Mother/(add name in print/sign above)   Date

NOTE: A copy of this document should be on file with the school and all staff members that interact with the above named student. The student should also have a copy on them at all times in case of emergencies.

DENIAL OR REVOCATION OF PREVIOUSLY AUTORIZATION TO BILL MEDICAID AND OR PEACHCARE FOR HEALTH RELATED SERVICES

Understanding the Impact: When Schools Bill Medicaid for Student Health Services
What It Means for Low-Income Families

The Hidden Costs: There are unintended consequences that can impact poor families:

- Medicaid Benefit Caps
  In some states, when schools bill Medicaid, those services may count against a child's annual Medicaid limit—potentially reducing access to medical care outside of school.

- Inadequate Consent & Communication
  Some families may sign Medicaid billing consent forms without fully understanding what's being shared or how it may affect their benefits.

- Privacy Risks
  Billing Medicaid involves sharing personal health data. If protections under FERPA and HIPAA aren't followed, families may face privacy violations or feel their trust has been breached.

- Overreliance on School-Based Care
  When school becomes the primary place a child receives healthcare, families may face a gap in services when the school year ends or if the child changes schools.

STATE OF _____
COUNTY OF_____

Parent/Student Name	]
Parent/Student Address	]
P/S, City/State/Zip	]
Parent/Legal Guardian	]
	] STUDENT NAME
To	] STUDENT DOB
School Name	]
School Address	]
School City/State/Zip	]
Respondent	]

DENIAL OR REVOCATION OF PREVIOUS AUTHORIZATION TO BILL MEDICAID AND/OR PEACHCARE FOR HEALTH RELATED SERVICES

PARENT NAME does not authorize NAME OF SCHOOL SYSTEM to bill Medicaid and/or PeachCare for health related services for STUDENT NAME in accordance with 34 CFR §300.154(d)(2)(i) that states: with regard to services required to provide FAPE (Free Appropriate Public Education) to an eligible child under this part, the public agency may NOT require parents to sign up for or enroll in public benefits or insurance programs in order for their child to receive FAPE under Part B of the Act (Individuals with Disabilities Education Act). I am not providing consent due to the risk of:

- decreased available lifetime coverage or any other insurance benefit (34 CFR §300.154(d)(2)(A))

- paying for services that would otherwise be covered by the public benefits or insurance program and that are required for the child outside of the time the child is in school (34 CFR §300.154(d)(2)(B))

-increase premiums or lead to the discontinuation of benefits or insurance (34 CFR §300.154(d)(2)(C))

-loss of eligibility for home and community-based waivers, based on aggregate health-related expenditures (34 CFR §300.154(d)(2)(D)).

I further understand that in accordance with 34 CFR §300.154(d)(2)(iv)(B) that my refusal to allow access to public benefits or insurance does NOT relieve the public agency of its responsibility to ensure that all required services are provided at NO COST to the parents.

_____   _____

Parent/Legal Guardian of Above Named Student   Date

A **Facilitated Individualized Education Program (IEP) meeting** is a special type of IEP meeting where a neutral, trained facilitator helps the IEP team work together collaboratively and productively. The goal is to create an IEP that best serves the student's needs while minimizing conflict among team members.

Key Aspects of a Facilitated IEP Meeting:
1. Neutral Facilitator – The facilitator is not a decision-maker but helps keep the meeting focused, ensures all voices are heard, and encourages problem-solving.
2. Collaboration & Communication – The facilitator helps the team work together respectfully, reducing tension and preventing disagreements from escalating.
3. Structured Process – The meeting follows a clear agenda to ensure all required topics are addressed without unnecessary delays or distractions.
4. Focus on the Student – The facilitator keeps the team centered on the student's needs, ensuring that discussions remain productive and solution-oriented.
5. Conflict Prevention – Facilitators use strategies to prevent misunderstandings and improve team dynamics, which can help avoid the need for formal dispute resolution.

When is a Facilitated IEP Meeting Used?
- When there is a history of tension or communication challenges among IEP team members.
- If parents or school staff feel that meetings are unproductive or overly contentious.
- As an alternative to mediation or due process when disagreements arise.

Who Provides the Facilitator?
- Some states offer free facilitation services through their Department of Education or special education agencies.
- Schools or parents may also hire an independent facilitator.

A Facilitated IEP Meeting is especially helpful in complex cases where strong emotions or differing perspectives make it hard to reach an agreement. It ensures the process stays fair, student-centered, and legally compliant.

To request a facilitated IEP meeting in GA you can ask for the form here: SPEDhelpdesk@doe.k12.ga.us. For all other states you should contact your states educational authority. A complete list of their websites are located in the appendix of this book.

Special education mediation is a voluntary and confidential process that helps resolve disputes between parents and school districts regarding a child's special education services under the Individuals with Disabilities Education Act (IDEA). It is designed to provide a collaborative, non-adversarial way to settle disagreements about issues such as evaluations, eligibility, Individualized Education Programs (IEPs), placement, or services.

Key Features of Special Education Mediation:
1. Voluntary Participation – Both the parents and the school district must agree to participate in mediation; neither party can be forced into it.
2. Neutral Mediator – A trained, impartial mediator facilitates the discussion. The mediator does not make decisions but helps both sides communicate effectively and find a mutually acceptable solution.
3. Confidentiality – Discussions in mediation cannot be used as evidence in future due process hearings or court cases, encouraging open and honest dialogue.
4. Free of Charge – Under IDEA, mediation must be provided at no cost to parents.
5. Legally Binding Agreement – If both parties reach an agreement, they sign a written document that is legally enforceable in court.

When Is Mediation Used?
Mediation can be used when parents and the school district disagree over:
- The child's eligibility for special education services
- The adequacy of an IEP or related services
- Placement decisions
- Discipline and behavior-related issues
- Any other disputes under IDEA

Advantages of Mediation
- Faster and Less Expensive than due process hearings or lawsuits.
- Less Adversarial, helping to maintain positive relationships between families and schools.
- More Collaborative, allowing both parties to have a say in the resolution.
- Flexible Solutions, since the agreement can be tailored to meet the student's needs.

To request mediation in GA download the form here: https://lor2.gadoe.org/gadoe/file/17cd61a8-53ce-4fa5-b818-6e856862814e/1/Procedures%20for%20Mediation.pdf

To find out whether mediation is available in your state just contact your state's educational authority, a complete list of websites is in the appendix of this book.

OPEN RECORDS/FREEDOM OF INFORMATION ACT

What Are Open Records?

"Open records" are documents, emails, reports, videos, and other materials created or held by government agencies that are not confidential under the law.

This can include:

- Meeting minutes
- Budgets and financial reports
- Police reports
- School district policies
- Contracts with vendors
- Public employee salaries (in most cases)

Who Must Comply?

- Federal agencies (under FOIA)
- State and local governments, including:
  - City councils
  - Police departments
  - School boards
  - Public universities Each state has its own open records law, and rules vary by state.

What's NOT Open?

Certain records are often excluded from public access to protect:

- Privacy (e.g., medical or student records)
- Ongoing investigations
- National security
- Trade secrets or proprietary business info
- Attorney-client communications

How to Request Open Records

1. Identify the agency holding the records.
2. Submit a formal request (some states require a specific format).
3. The agency must respond within a set time (varies by state).
4. They can provide the records, deny the request (with a legal reason), or charge a fee for copying or research.

Why It Matters

- Promotes government transparency
- Allows citizens and journalists to investigate issues
- Helps ensure accountability and trust

STATE OF GEORGIA
COUNTY OF _____

NAME OF REQUESTOR	]	FACILITY NAME
Address	]	Address
City/State/Zip	]	City State Zip
Email address	]	Email address
Phone number	]	phone number
Public Record Requester	]	Public Record Holder

GEORGIA OPEN RECORDS ACT- O.C.G.A. § 50-18-70-REQUEST FOR ACCESS

The Public Record Requester ask for access to inspect and copy the following public records, including any public electronic records:

- (INSERT A DETAILED DESCRIPTION OF THE RECORDS WITH DATES)

As the Georgia Open Records Act requires, please let Public Record Requester know if search, copying, retrieval and/or digital media copying fees are estimated to exceed $25.

If the records request is denied, in whole or in part, please provide Public Record Requester with the section of the Act on which the denial or redaction is based. In cases where a portion of the data and/or document(s) is exempt, please redact that portion and release the remainder.

If the document(s) exists in electronic format, the Public Record Requester ask that they be provided in electronic form, in accordance with the Act. Public Record Requester looks forward to a response no later than <u>three (3) working days from today</u>.

Please contact the Public Record Requester if clarification is needed to fulfill this request or if there are easier ways for the Public Record Requester to get the information the requested

In the interest of timeliness, Public Record Requester ask that no contact by postal mail be attempted. Public Record Requester's email is *EMAIL@EMAIL.COM*, and Public Record Requester's phone for call/text is *123.456.7890*

_____

Signature of Above Public Record Requester   Date of Request

Above is a form for the Georgia Open Records Act. Every state has similar laws and likely sample forms. All 50 states laws are in the appendix of this book. https://www.nfoic.org/state-sample-foia-request-letters/

STATE OF _____
COUNTY OF _____

NAME OF REQUESTOR	]	FACILITY NAME
Address	]	Address
City/State/Zip	]	City State Zip
Email address	]	Email address
Phone number	]	phone number
Public Record Requester	]	Public Record Holder

FREEDOM OF INFORMATION ACT- 5 USC § 552-REQUEST FOR ACCESS

The request for preservation and production of records dated (DATE/TIME) is made pursuant to the Freedom of Information Act 5 USC § 552. Records requested include:

RECORD DESCRIPTION BETWEEN DATES ???-???

In order to help determine my status for the purpose of assessing fees, you should know that I am: *(delete what does not apply)*-

-A REPRESENTATIVE OF THE NEWS MEDIA AFFILIATED WITH THE ???? NEWS ORGANIZATION AND THIS REQUEST IS MADE AS PART OF NEWS GATHERING AND NOT FOR COMMERCIAL USE;
-AFFILIATED WITH AN EDUCATONAL OR NONCOMMERCIAL SCIENTIFIC INSTITUTION, AND THIS REQUEST IS MADE FOR A SCHOLARLY OR SCIENTIFIC PURPOSE AND NOT FOR A COMMERCIAL USE;
-AFFILIATED WITH A PRIVATE BUSINESS AND AM SEEKING INFORMATION FOR USE IN THE COMPANY'S BUSINESS

I request a waiver of all fees for this request. Disclosure of the requested information to me is in the public interest because it is likely to contribute significantly to the public understanding of the operations or activities of the government and is not primarily in my commercial interest. The information will be synthesized and disseminated by the requestor for public benefit. In the alternative I am willing to pay a fee of no more than $????, but if you estimate the cost will be in excess of this amount contact me first.

The information requested is expected to be provided within 30 days of the date of request below.

If you have any questions about handling this request you may contact me:

     Email   INSERT EMAIL ADDRESS

     Call/Text: INSERT CELL PHONE NUMBER

_____   _____

Signature of Above Requester   Date of Request

STATE OF _____
COUNTY OF _____

PARENT/GUARDIAN NAME	]
Address	]
City-State-Zip	]
Parent/Legal Guardian	]
	]
	] STUDENT NAME
To	] DOB-00/00/0000
	]
TEACHER NAME/SPED DIRECTOR NAME	]
Name of School/School System	]
School System Address	]
School City-State-Zip	]
Respondent	]

PETITION TO OBSERVE STUDENT CLASSROOM

Be advised that the confidentiality requirements in the Family Educational Rights and Privacy Act (FERPA) only relate to education records and DO NOT prohibit parental observations of the classroom.

Observation of my child's classroom is necessary for me to be a fully informed and equal member of the IEP team. Therefore in accordance with the Individuals with Disabilities Act and my parental obligation, I ask that you contact me at your earliest convenience but no later than 10 days from the date of this document so the observation can be scheduled at a mutually agreeable time.

_____   _____

Parent/Legal Guardian of Above Named Student   Date

STATE OF _____
COUNTY OF _____

PARENT NAME(S)	]
Parent Address	]
Parent City/State/Zip	]
Parent Phone Number	]
Parent Email Address	]
Parent/Guardian	]
	] STUDENT NAME
To	] DATE OF BIRTH
_____COUNTY SCHOOL	]
School Address	]
School City/State/Zip	]

PROHIBITION OF AVERSIVE INTERVENTIONS, RESTRAINT, AND SECLUSIONS

We are writing to formally document our position regarding the use of aversive interventions, restraint, or seclusion in relation to our child, [Student's Name], a student at [School Name]. [Student's Name] has been identified as a student with [Name of Disabilities] and receives special education services pursuant to the Individuals with Disabilities Education Act (IDEA).

We have serious concerns that [Student's Name]'s behavioral challenges may be, or in the future could be, addressed through the use of aversive techniques, physical restraint, seclusion (including seclusionary time-out), or any other procedure euphemistically referred to as "physical management" or "restrictive procedures." Such practices include, but are not limited to: forcible holds or dragging, the use of ties or straps, chemical or mechanical restraints, facial sprays, physical striking, deliberate humiliation, deprivation of nutrition or exercise, and the use of time-out rooms in a punitive or excessive manner.

This letter serves as formal notice that we do not authorize, and expressly withhold our consent for, the use of any of these procedures on our child while at school, during school-sponsored activities, or while being transported to or from school. The use of any such methods on [Student's Name] will be considered a violation of our parental rights and [Student's Name]'s rights under applicable federal and state laws.

Pursuant to IDEA, when a student exhibits challenging behaviors, the school is required to conduct a Functional Behavioral Assessment (FBA) and implement a Positive Behavior Support (PBS) plan to address the behaviors in a lawful and constructive manner. If [Student's Name]'s behavior is deemed sufficiently challenging to warrant consideration of aversive or restrictive procedures, seclusion, time-out, or physical management, then it is evident that an FBA must be conducted, and a comprehensive PBS plan must be developed. We expect to fully participate in both the assessment process and the development of an effective PBS plan to ensure that [Student's Name]'s needs are addressed in a lawful and appropriate manner.

There have been numerous reports of injuries, trauma, and even fatalities of children with disabilities subjected to aversive interventions, restraint, and seclusion. This letter is a precautionary measure to prevent any such harm to our child. If any of these techniques are currently in use or have been used in the past with [Student's Name], we require immediate written notification, along with all relevant documentation, and demand the immediate cessation of such practices.

If [Student's Name] exhibits behavioral challenges now or in the future, we request that a behavior support team meeting be convened to discuss the concerns, initiate an FBA across environments, and develop a positive behavior intervention plan. We invoke our right to participate in all such meetings.

Furthermore, in the event of an emergency in which school personnel feel unequipped to respond in a safe and non-threatening manner, we direct that the following family members be contacted rather than resorting to restraint, seclusion, or law enforcement intervention:

Parent Name	Phone Number
Parent Name	Phone Number

We seek to collaborate with [School Name] staff, teachers, and professionals to ensure that [Student's Name] develops appropriate behavioral skills in a safe and supportive environment. Like you, we are committed to ensuring that [Student's Name]'s school is a secure learning environment for all students and staff. We look forward to working together to achieve this goal.

Please confirm receipt of this letter in writing and provide a response outlining the school's policies and assurances regarding the matters addressed herein.

Sincerely,

[Parent(s) Name(s)]

PARENT SIGNATURE   DATE

Cc: Superintendent, Principal, anyone else that interacts with the student

State laws regarding the denial of recess as a disciplinary measure vary across the United States. Some states have enacted legislation to ensure that recess cannot be withheld as punishment, while others leave such decisions to local school districts. Below is an overview of the policies in various states:

STATES WITH LAWS PROHIBITING WITHHOLDING RECESS AS PUNISHMENT:
Illinois: In 2021, Illinois passed a law requiring all public schools to provide 30 minutes of daily unstructured free time to K-5 students. This law explicitly prohibits withholding recess as a disciplinary measure, except when a student's participation poses an immediate threat to safety.
New Jersey: State law stipulates that schools cannot withhold recess more than twice per week and only for violations of the district's student code of conduct.
Rhode Island: Legislation encourages teachers to make a "good-faith effort" not to withhold recess for disciplinary reasons.

STATES WITH LAWS MANDATING RECESS BUT NO SPECIFIC PROHIBITION ON WITHHOLDING
States with Laws Mandating Recess but No Specific Prohibition on Withholding:
California: Starting in the 2024-2025 school year, all public school children are required to have 30 minutes of daily recess.
Louisiana: As of August 1, 2023, schools must provide at least one 15-minute recess period daily.
Washington: Beginning with the 2024-2025 school year, a law requires 30 minutes of daily recess for students.
Georgia: In 2023, Georgia enacted a law requiring daily recess for most elementary students but does not specify the duration or address withholding recess as a disciplinary measure.

STATES ENCOURAGING RECESS WITHOUT SPECIFIC MANDATES:
Minnesota: The state is refining the definition of recess retention and stipulating circumstances under which withholding recess is acceptable.
Connecticut: The State Board of Education recommends that local boards establish policies promoting physical activity, including recess, but there is no formal law mandating it.

STATES WITHOUT SPECIFIC RECESS POLICIES:
Several states do not have explicit laws or policies regarding recess or the withholding of recess as a disciplinary measure. In these states, decisions are typically made at the local school district level. For instance, as of 2010, states like Arizona, Delaware, Florida, and Georgia had no general physical activity requirements or policies requiring or recommending recess or physical activity breaks.

GENERAL OBSERVATIONS:
-While some states have taken legislative action to mandate recess and prohibit its use as a disciplinary tool, many others leave these decisions to local jurisdictions.
-Advocacy groups continue to push for more comprehensive policies to ensure that all students have access to regular recess, recognizing its importance for physical and mental health.

For the most current information, it's advisable to consult state education departments or local school district policies, as laws and regulations can change over time. A list of all 50 State Educational Authorities are in the appendix of this book.

STATE OF GEORGIA
COUNTY OF _____

PARENT NAME   ]
Parent/Student Address   ]
Parent City/State/Zip   ]
Parent Phone   ]
Parent Email Address   ]
   Parent/Legal Guardian   ]
                                          ]   STUDENT NAME
                  To   ]   STUDENT DOB
SCHOOL DISTRICT NAME   ]
School Address   ]
School City/State/Zip   ]
School Phone   ]
School Email   ]
   Respondent   ]

OF OCGA 20-2-323-RECESS FOR STUDENTS IN KINDERGARTEN THROUGH GRADE FIVE; UNSTRUCTURED BREAK TIME FOR STUDENTS IN KINDERGARDEN THROUGH GRADE EIGHT

(a) Beginning in the 2022-2023 school year, each elementary school shall schedule recess for all students in kindergarten and grades one through five every school day; provided, however, that recess shall not be required on any school day on which a student has had physical education or structured activity time or if reasonable circumstances impede such recess, such as inclement weather when no indoor space is available, assemblies or field trips exceeding their scheduled duration, conflicts occurring at the scheduled recess time over which the classroom teacher has no control, or emergencies, disasters, or acts of God.

(b) Each local board of education shall establish written policies allowing unstructured break time for students in kindergarten and grades one through eight. The policies shall include, but shall not be limited to, the following matters:

    (1) The school personnel who will be authorized to decide the length, frequency, timing, and location of breaks;

    (2) Whether breaks can be withheld from students for disciplinary or academic reasons and, if breaks can be withheld, under what conditions;

    (3) How to ensure break time is a safe experience for students, including the responsibility for supervision of students; and

    (4) How to ensure that break time is scheduled so as to provide a support for academic learning.

Local boards shall provide a copy of such policies to the State Board of Education.

The above named parent request a copy of these policies be provided within _10 days_ of the date of this notice.

_____   _____
PARENT SIGNATURE   DATE

One-Party Consent States

In these states, only one person involved in the conversation needs to consent to the recording. If *you* are part of the conversation, you can legally record it without informing the others.

Examples of One-Party Consent States (not exhaustive):

- New York
- Texas
- Florida
- Illinois
- New Jersey
- Georgia
- Ohio
- Pennsylvania *(see note below)*
- Michigan *(gray area — varies depending on circumstances)*

Two-Party (or All-Party) Consent States

In these states, all parties involved in a private conversation must consent to the recording. Secretly recording someone without their consent is typically illegal.

Two-Party (All-Party) Consent States (as of current laws):

- California
- Florida*
- Maryland
- Massachusetts
- Montana
- Nevada
- New Hampshire
- Pennsylvania*
- Washington
- Connecticut (in-person conversations require all-party consent)

Note: Florida and Pennsylvania are often labeled "two-party," but courts have interpreted their laws differently at times. It's safest to treat them as all-party consent.

Federal Law

Under federal law, only one party needs to consent. However, if you're in a two-party consent state, the stricter law applies.

Things to Consider

- Private vs. public: Consent laws generally apply to *private* conversations. Conversations held in public spaces where there is no expectation of privacy may not be protected.
- Cross-state calls: If you're recording a call between two states, the safest bet is to follow the stricter state law.
- Civil and criminal penalties: Violations can result in lawsuits, fines, or even criminal charges.

STATE OF _____
COUNTY OF _____

Parent/Student Name]	
Parent/Student Address]	
P/S, City/State/Zip]	
Parent/Legal Guardian]	
]	STUDENT NAME
To]	STUDENT DOB
School Name]	
School Address]	
School City/State/Zip]	
Respondent]	

NOTICE OF INTENT TO RECORD

This is to inform you that, pursuant to rights as stated at (**OCGA 16-11-66**) quoted below, the meeting scheduled for (DATE OF MEETING) will be recorded using the Otter.ai application. We encourage all participants to record the meeting using a device of their choice.

**OCGA 16-11-66

   (a) **Nothing in Code Section 16-11-62 shall prohibit a person from intercepting a wire, oral, or electronic communication where such person is a party to the communication or one of the parties to the communication has given prior consent to such interception.**

Upon request, a transcript and recording will be made available to school personnel immediately after the meeting. Please include this notice in the student's permanent educational record

Respectfully Submitted,
PARENT NAME

****DISCLAIMER:** The law cited is Georgia law and the rules and penalties for recording vary by state. To check the law in your state: https://www.justia.com/documents/50-state-surveys-recording-calls-and-conversations.pdf

STATE OF _____
COUNTY OF _____

Parent/Student Name	]
Parent/Student Address	]
P/S, City/State/Zip	]
Parent/Legal Guardian	]
	] STUDENT NAME
To	] STUDENT DOB
School Name	]
School Address	]
School City/State/Zip	]
Respondent	]

REQUEST FOR INDEPENDENT EVALUATION

This document serves as request for an independent evaluation of the above named student at public expense in accordance 34 CFR 300.502(a)(3)(ii) that states: Public expense means that the public agency either pays for the full cost of the evaluation or ensures that the evaluation is otherwise provided at no cost to the parent, consistent with §300.301-Initial Evaluations. The following specific independent evaluations are requested:

HEARING/VISION

SOCIAL/EMOTIONAL

ACHIEVEMENT/INTELLIGENCE COMPREHENSIVE PSYCHO-EDUCATIONAL EVAL

SPEECH/LANGUAGE EVALUATION-COMPREHENSIVE

COMMUNICATION EVALUATION BY A SPEECH LANGUAGE PATHOLOGIST

FUNCTIONAL BEHAVIORAL ASSESSMENT BY A BOARD CERTIFIED BEHAVIORAL ANALYST

MOTOR/OCCUPATIONAL THERPAY EVALUATION

ASSISTIVE DEVICE EVALUATION

WRAP AROUND SERVICES AND RESIDENTIAL PLACEMENT EVALUATION

VOCATIONAL REHABILITATION

In accordance with §300.502(b)(4): If a parent requests an independent educational evaluation, the public agency may ask for the parent's reason why he or she objects to the public evaluation. However, the public agency may not require the parent to provide an explanation and may not unreasonably delay either providing the independent educational evaluation at public expense or filing a due process complaint to request a due process hearing to defend the public evaluation.

Because the evaluation was performed by the public agency it is inherently biased and an independent evaluation by an unbiased third party is requested for comparison purposes. Additional reasons for the request are declined. Approval of the request along with any district requirements for the independent evaluation is expected within ten (10) days of the date of this signed and delivered request. Otherwise it is expected that within ten (10) days the above name respondent will file a due process complaint in accordance with §300.502(b)(2)(i) that states: If a parent request an independent educational evaluation at public expense, the public agency must, without unnecessary delay file a due process complaint to request a hearing to show that its evaluation is appropriate.

_____   _____

Parent/Legal Guardian of Above Named Student   Date of Consent

STATE OF _____
COUNTY OF _____

Parent/Student Name]	
Parent/Student Address]	
P/S, City/State/Zip]	
Parent/Legal Guardian]	
]	STUDENT
NAME]	
To]	STUDENT DOB
School Name]	
School Address]	
School City/State/Zip]	
Respondent]	

REQUEST FOR PRIOR WRITTEN NOTICE

This document serves as request for prior written notice regarding the above named student in accordance with 34 CFR §300.503(a) Notice: Written notice that meets the requirements of paragraph (b) of this section must be given to the parents of a child with a disability a reasonable time before the public agency-(1) Proposes to initiate or change the identification, evaluation, or educational placement of the child or the provision of FAPE to the child; or (2) Refuses to initiate or change the identification, evaluation, or educational placement of the child or the provision of FAPE to the child.

Prior written notice regarding (Insert the issue specific to your child) is expected within **_ten days (10)_** of the date of this signed document. In accordance with §300.503(b) Content.of notice. The prior written notice should include:

(1) A description of the action proposed or refused by the agency;

(2) An explanation of why the agency proposes or refuses to take the action;

(3) A description of each evaluation procedure, assessment, record, or report the agency used as a basis for the proposed or refused action;

(4) A statement that the parents of a child with a disability have protection under the procedural safeguards of this part and, if this notice is not an initial referral for evaluation, the means by which a copy of a description of the procedural safeguards can be obtained;

(5) Sources for parents to contact to obtain assistance in understanding the provisions of this part;

(6) A description of other options that the IEP Team considered and the reasons why those options were rejected; and

(7) A description of other factors that are relevant to the agency's proposal or refusal.

_____   _____
Parent/Legal Guardian of Above Named Student   Date

STATE OF _____
COUNTY OF _____

Parent/Student Name   ]
Parent/Student Address   ]
P/S, City/State/Zip   ]
   Parent/Legal Guardian   ]
                            ]   STUDENT NAME
           To   ]   STUDENT DOB
School Name   ]
School Address   ]
School City/State/Zip   ]
   Respondent   ]
                            ]

REQUIRED ACCOMMODATIONS NOTICE

This is to inform you that, pursuant to rights as stated under the Americans with Disabilities Act, the following accommodations are needed for full access to the scheduled Individualized Education Meeting scheduled for (DATE OF MEETING):

INTERPRETER (for example)
-(ACCOMMODATION 2)
-(ACCOMMODATION 3)

20 USC 12182:

    No individual shall be discriminated against on the basis of disability in the full and equal enjoyment of the goods, services, facilities, privileges, advantages, or accommodations of any place of public accommodation by any person who owns, leases (or leases to), or operates a place of public accommodation

Please confirm with me on or before (DATE) whether the above accommodations will be available for the meeting so that I can am able to fully and equally participate.

Respectfully Submitted,
PARENT NAME

Retaining students (i.e., holding them back to repeat a grade) is not considered an effective practice for most students, especially those with learning or behavioral challenges.

Here's why:

What the Research Says:
- The National Association of School Psychologists (NASP) and other professional organizations strongly discourage retention because it's associated with:
  - Lower academic achievement over time
  - Increased risk of dropping out
  - Social and emotional issues (like shame, low self-esteem, and disengagement)
  - Disproportionate use on students of color, students with disabilities, and those from low-income backgrounds
- Studies have shown that the short-term gains from retention often fade within 2–3 years, and retained students often continue to struggle academically.

What's More Effective:
- Targeted interventions: individualized instruction, tutoring, and academic support tailored to the student's needs.
- MTSS/RTI frameworks: Multi-Tiered Systems of Support or Response to Intervention help identify struggling students early and provide appropriate support.
- Special education evaluations when warranted to determine if a learning disability or other issue is affecting progress.
- Accommodations and modifications: changes to the learning environment, assignments, or expectations that support access and success.

Bottom line:
Retention is often a reactive, not proactive, response to academic struggles. Rather than fixing the root of the problem, it delays it — and can cause more harm in the long run.

RETENTION QUESTIONS

1   Why are you recommending retention when it's a practice proven to be harmful, according to the National Association of School Psychologists? Are you ignoring the research, or just choosing to gamble with my child's future?

2.   How did you allow my child to fail an entire academic year without stepping in with effective services, supports, or accommodations? This is not just negligence — it's a complete failure of your legal and professional responsibilities.

3.   You really expect my child to repeat the *same* grade, using the *same* failed instructional methods, and somehow believe the outcome will be *different*? That's not just ineffective — it's irrational.

4.   Give me one good reason why I shouldn't file a complaint against your license and inform my state senator and representative. Taxpayer-funded schools should not be allowed to treat students with disabilities this way — and I will make sure others are made aware.

SCHOOL CHOICE OPTIONS

IN DISTRICT TRANSFERS

Some states allow students to transfer to other schools within their district. To determine whether your state allows transfers check your state's educational authority. A list of all 50 state's websites are in the appendix of this book. Because I practice in Georgia I will highlight how it works in this state along with a request form. Your state likely has something similar.

Georgia's HB 251 Public School Choice law allows parents to request a transfer for their child to another public school within their local school district, provided space is available. Here's how it works:

Eligibility & Process:

1. Who Can Apply?
   o Parents of students enrolled in Georgia public schools.
2. Transfer Options:
   o Students can transfer to another public school within their district if there is available classroom space.
3. Application Process:
   o Each school district sets its own application window and process for HB 251 transfers.
   o Parents must submit a transfer request within the designated period.
4. Approval Criteria:
   o Approval is based on class size availability—districts are not required to exceed capacity limits.
   o Some schools may have more applicants than available seats, in which case a lottery system may be used.
5. Transportation:
   o Parents are responsible for providing transportation to and from the new school.
6. Special Considerations:
   o Schools may deny transfers if they do not have the resources to meet the student's needs (e.g., special education services may vary by school).
   o The student can remain at the new school until completing the highest grade level offered there.

Key Takeaways:
- HB 251 does not allow students to transfer between different districts.
- Space availability is the biggest factor in approval.
- Parents must provide their own transportation.
- Transfer policies and deadlines vary by district.

_____ COUNTY SCHOOL SYSTEM

HOUSE BILL 251 SCHOOL YEAR _____

Complete The Form & Mail It To Your Local Board Of Education Office

Deadline for Applications _____ (varies by district)

Date of Notification of Enrollment Decision _____ (varies by district)

Under a 2009 state law (O.C.G.A. § 20-2-2131), parents may request a transfer to another public school within their local school district. If you wish to request a transfer, please complete the information below. '

Parent Transfer Request Form (Parent Must Complete)

Date_____Student Name_____Grade_____

Grade Level for Fall(Year)_____Birthdate_____Age_____

_____County Student Identification Number_____

Name of Custodial Parent/Guardian Requesting Transfer_____

Home Address:_____City_____State_____Zip_____

Phone_____Email_____

Name of Student' Currently Zoned School_____

Parent Request for School Transfer

I (Name of Parent/Guardian)_____am requesting a

Transfer for (Student Name)_____to attend one of the

following schools in the district if space is available:

Parent/Guardian Ranked List of Schools for Transfer when more than one school is available:

First Choice_____

Second Choice_____

Third Choice_____

IN DISTRICT & OUT OF DISTRICT TRANSFERS & PRIVATE SCHOOL FUNDING

Some states allow students to transfer to other schools within outside of their district. To determine whether your state allows transfers check your state's educational authority. A list of all 50 state's websites are in the appendix of this book. Because I practice in Georgia I will highlight how it works in this state. Your state may have something similar.

Georgia's Special Needs Scholarship Program (SB10) is a school choice program that allows parents of students with disabilities to use state funds to attend a participating private school or another public school that better meets their child's needs. Here's a breakdown of how it works:

Eligibility Requirements:
1. Residency – The student must be a Georgia resident.
2. IEP or 504 Plan – The student must have an Individualized Education Program (IEP) or a Section 504 Plan related to specific disabilities.
3. Public School Attendance – The student must have been enrolled in a Georgia public school the prior school year (exceptions exist for military families).

How It Works:
- Parents can apply for a scholarship to help cover tuition and fees at an approved private school that participates in the program.
- Alternatively, parents can transfer their child to another public school within or outside their district if the school has space and agrees to accept the student.

Funding:
- The scholarship amount varies based on the student's level of special education services.
- The amount is typically a portion of the state funds that would have been allocated to the student in public school.

Key Considerations:
- The program does not guarantee placement in a specific private or public school.
- Parents are responsible for any tuition or fees that exceed the scholarship amount.
- Some private schools may have admissions requirements or may not provide all the services a student needs.

More information and a list of public schools can be found here: https://www.gadoe.org/External-Affairs-and-Policy/Policy/Pages/Special-Needs-Scholarship-Program.aspx

To determine the amount of funding your child is entitled to use the calculator that can be found here: https://finance.doe.k12.ga.us/ScholarshipPublicWeb/EligibilityCalculator.aspx?pagevalue=2

The Georgia GOAL Scholarship Program is a tax credit scholarship program that helps students attend private schools by using contributions from individuals and businesses who receive a state tax credit in return. It was created under Georgia's Qualified Education Expense (QEE) Tax Credit Program. Contact your state's educational authority to see if there is something similar in your state. A list of all 50 can be found in this book's appendix.

How It Works:
1. Taxpayers Donate – Individuals and businesses contribute to the Georgia GOAL Scholarship Program instead of paying that amount in state income taxes.
2. Tax Credit – Donors receive a dollar-for-dollar Georgia state tax credit for their contributions (up to specific limits).
3. Scholarships for Students – GOAL uses these funds to provide scholarships to K-12 students so they can attend participating private schools.

Who Is Eligible for a GOAL Scholarship?
- Students must be Georgia residents.
- The student must be enrolling in a private school for the first time or transferring from a public school.
- The family must meet income eligibility requirements (typically based on a percentage of the federal poverty level).

Donation Limits for Taxpayers:
- Individuals – Up to $2,500
- Married Couples – Up to $5,000
- Businesses (Pass-through Entities) – Up to $25,000 or 75% of Georgia tax liability
- C-Corporations & Fiduciaries – Up to 75% of Georgia tax liability

Key Benefits:
- For Families – Allows students to access private school education that better fits their needs.
- For Donors – Provides a 100% state tax credit while supporting education.
- For Private Schools – Increases accessibility for students who may not afford tuition otherwise.

More information about GOAL can be found here:
https://www.goalscholarship.org/for_parents/page/scholarship-process

A list of participating schools can be found here:
https://www.goalscholarship.org/participating_schools/

EDUCATION SAVINGS ACCOUNTS

The Georgia Promise Scholarship Program, established in 2024, is designed to provide eligible families in Georgia with financial assistance to pursue alternative educational opportunities for their children. Contact your state's educational authority to see if there is something similar in your state. A list of all 50 can be found in this book's appendix. Here's an overview of how The Georgia Promise Scholarship Program works:

Eligibility Criteria:
- Current Enrollment: Students must have been enrolled in a Georgia public school for two consecutive semesters immediately preceding their application.
- Rising Kindergarteners: Students entering kindergarten are also eligible.
- Residency in Designated Zones: The student must reside in the attendance zone of a public school identified by the Governor's Office of Student Achievement as being in the bottom 25% based on academic performance.
- Parental Residency: Parents or guardians must have been residents of Georgia for at least one year prior to applying, with exceptions made for active-duty military families.
- Application Process:
- Application Period: The online application portal opens on March 1 and closes on April 15, 2025.
- Submission: Families can apply through the official website.
- Notification: Applicants will be informed of their acceptance into the program after the application window closes.

Scholarship Details:
- Funding Amount: Each eligible student may receive up to $6,500 for the 2025–2026 academic year.
- Administrative Fees: The Georgia Education Savings Authority (GESA) may withhold up to 5% of the scholarship amount for administrative purposes.

Approved Uses of Funds:
- Private School Tuition and Fees: Payment for tuition and associated fees at participating private schools.
- Tutoring Services: Services provided by educators certified by the Georgia Professional Standards Commission.
- Therapeutic Services: Occupational, behavioral, physical, or speech-language therapies provided by licensed professionals.
- Curriculum and Educational Materials: Purchase of textbooks, supplemental materials, and approved curricula.
- Transportation: Up to $500 annually for transportation expenses to approved service providers.

Priority Considerations:
- Income Level: Students from families with an income not exceeding 400% of the federal poverty level receive priority.
- Continued Participation: Students who have previously received the scholarship are prioritized over new applicants in subsequent years.

Ongoing Eligibility:
Once accepted, students remain eligible until they return to public school, graduate from high school, reach the age of 20 (21 for special education students), or move out of Georgia. For more detailed information and to access the application portal, please visit the official Georgia Promise Scholarship website: mygeorgiapromise.org.

CHARTER SCHOOLS

Charter schools are publicly funded but independently operated schools that function under a contract (or "charter") with a state, district, or other authorizing body. They were created to provide alternatives to traditional public schools and are designed to have more flexibility in their operations in exchange for greater accountability for performance.

Key Features of Charter Schools:

1. Publicly Funded, Independently Operated – Charter schools receive government funding like traditional public schools but are run by independent boards, non-profits, or even for-profit organizations, depending on state laws.

2. Flexibility – They have more autonomy in their curriculum, staffing, scheduling, and teaching methods than district-run schools, which allows for innovation and specialization.

3. Accountability – Charter schools must meet the academic and operational benchmarks outlined in their charter agreement. If they fail to meet expectations, they can be shut down.

4. Open Enrollment – They are tuition-free and must accept all students, but if demand exceeds available seats, they typically use a lottery system for admissions.

5. Varying State Laws – Each state has its own laws governing charter schools, including how they are funded, how they are authorized, and what regulations they must follow.

6. Performance Variability – While some charter schools excel, others may struggle with academic performance, funding, or governance issues.

7. Charter schools must comply with federal laws like the Individuals with Disabilities Education Act (IDEA) and Section 504 of the Rehabilitation Act, ensuring that students with disabilities receive appropriate services. However, there are concerns about whether charter schools provide the same level of support as traditional public schools.

Both the State Charter Schools Commission of Georgia and Georgia Charter Schools Association both can provide more information regarding specific charter schools in the state. You can find their websites here: https://scsc.georgia.gov & https://gacharters.org.

Many local school districts provide information about charter schools operating within their jurisdiction. Contact your state or local educational authority to see if there is something similar. A list of all 50 website state educational authorities can be found in this book's appendix.

HOMESCHOOLING

Homeschooling is an education model where parents or guardians take primary responsibility for teaching their children at home instead of sending them to a traditional public or private school. It offers flexibility in curriculum, pace, and teaching methods to suit a child's learning style and needs.

Key Aspects of Homeschooling
1. Legal Requirements – Each U.S. state has its own homeschooling laws, including notification requirements, record-keeping, and assessments.
2. Curriculum Choice – Parents can choose from various curricula, including traditional textbooks, online programs, or self-designed lesson plans.
3. Parental Responsibility – Parents serve as primary educators but can use tutors, co-ops, or online classes for additional support.
4. Flexibility – Homeschooling allows for a personalized education pace and schedule, accommodating travel, special needs, or unique learning styles.
5. Socialization – Homeschooled students often engage in co-ops, extracurricular activities, community programs, or sports teams to interact with peers.

Homeschooling & Special Education
- Parents homeschooling children with special needs must arrange for their own therapy and support services.
- Some states allow access to public school resources like speech therapy or Individualized Education Program (IEP) services, but Georgia has limited options for homeschoolers.
- Georgia's Special Needs Scholarship (SB10) allows students with IEPs to use state funds for private education but does not apply to homeschooling.

Homeschooling in Georgia
Georgia allows parents to homeschool but requires:
- A Declaration of Intent to homeschool filed annually with the Georgia Department of Education.
- Instruction of at least 180 days per year, 4.5 hours per day.
- A basic curriculum covering reading, math, science, social studies, and language arts.
- Standardized testing every three years beginning in third grade (results are for parental records only).
- Annual progress reports maintained but not submitted to the state.

For more information about Homeschooling in Georgia:
Georgia Department of Education: https://gadoe.org/parent-family-resources/home-school/
Georgia Home Education Association: https://ghea.org/?utm_source=chatgpt.com

For Homeschooling resources consult your state's educational authority. All 50 websites can be found in the appendix of this book.

VIRTUAL SCHOOL

Virtual school, also known as online school, is an educational model where students complete their coursework through digital platforms instead of attending a physical classroom. These schools can be fully online or blended (combining online and in-person instruction).

Key Features of Virtual Schools

1. Online Learning Platform – Students access lessons, assignments, and tests via an online portal. Classes may be live (synchronous) or self-paced (asynchronous).
2. Certified Teachers – Most virtual schools have state-certified instructors who provide instruction, grade assignments, and offer support.
3. Flexible Schedule – Students can often complete work on their own time, making virtual school ideal for those needing a non-traditional schedule.
4. Accreditation & Accountability – Many virtual schools are state-approved and follow curriculum guidelines similar to traditional schools.
5. Parental Involvement – Parents may serve as learning coaches, especially in elementary and middle school grades.

Types of Virtual Schools

1. Public Virtual Schools – Tuition-free programs run by state education departments or local school districts (e.g., Georgia Virtual School).
2. Charter Virtual Schools – Online charter schools that operate independently but follow state education laws.
3. Private Virtual Schools – Tuition-based programs that offer specialized or religious-based online education.
4. Supplemental Online Courses – Students in traditional schools can take online classes to supplement their in-person education.

Virtual School in Georgia

Georgia offers several virtual learning options, including:

- Georgia Virtual School (GaVS) is a state-run program offering tuition-free middle and high school courses. Website: https://www.gavirtualschool.org/
- Georgia Cyber Academy (GCA) is a full-time, tuition-free online charter school for K-12 students. Website: https://www.georgiacyber.org/
- Connections Academy is a tuition-free, state-approved virtual public school option. Website: https://www.connectionsacademy.com/
- Private Virtual Schools are various accredited private online programs for Georgia students.
  Website: https://ghea.org/

To find more information about virtual school in your state consult your state educational authority. All 50 states websites are in the appendix of this book.

SPECIFIC POWER OF ATTORNEY FOR EDUCATIONAL DECISIONS

Student:_____DOB:_____ID#:_____Date:_____

I, (*STUDENT NAME*), born on (*STUDENT –DOB*), hereby make, constitute and appoint (*PARENT/GUARDIAN NAME*), my (*PARENT/GUARDIAN RELATIONSHIP*), as my Agent to act in my name, place and stead, make all educational decisions on my behalf, act and legally bind me to any and all educational decisions and or programs, including, but not limited to, the following hereinafter described:

(initial) _____ receive notice of all meetings and actions proposed or refused pertinent to my special education program;

(initial) _____ participate in all meetings and conferences pertaining to me

(initial) _____ requests legal due process proceedings if a disagreement regarding my special education program arises

(initial) _____ represent my interest in mediation to resolve disputes with the local school division

(initial) _____ agree or disagree with proposed individualized education programs and special education placements

(initial) _____ to enroll me in any educational programs

(initial) _____ to authorize any services for me that are designed to provide me with educational Benefit and/or access to a free appropriate public education as provided for in the Individuals with Disabilities Education Act.

(initial) _____ to negotiate and approve on my behalf reasonable accommodations in educational services as required under Section 504 of the Rehabilitation Act of 1973.

(initial) _____ to have access to my school records and other personal education information. The scope of this power shall also extend to confidential records and information, whether prepared by school personnel or by third parties, including but not limited to medical services providers, psychological services providers, assistive technology providers, speech, physical and occupational services providers, social work providers, and any provider of durable medical equipment.

(initial) _____ to investigate and arrange for opportunities for me to engage in educational activities that provide occupational training.

as I would, might or could do if acting personally. I hereby ratify and confirm all lawful acts done by said Agent in accordance with this specific power of attorney. This specific power of attorney shall not terminate upon me becoming disabled, incompetent, or incapacitated, and all power and authority granted here under to said Agent shall continue and be exercisable by said Agent notwithstanding that I may subsequently become disabled, incompetent, or incapacitated, and all acts done by said Agent pursuant to this specific power of attorney during the period of any such disability, incompetence, or incapacity, shall have in all respects, the same effect and shall inure to the benefits and bind me and my estate fully.

REVOCATION OF POWER OF ATTORNEY

I may revoke the Specific Power of Attorney for Educational Decisions by a writing signed and dated by me.

RELEASE OF THIRD PARTIES

In the absence of actual notice that I have revoked this instrument, no person, school district or its personnel, organization, corporation, or other entity who deals with my Agent shall incur any liability to me, my estate, my heirs, or my assigns for permitting or facilitating my Agent in the exercise of the authority granted under this instrument. I hereby release all such persons, organizations, corporations, or other entities from any liability arising from their reliance on this instrument.

PHOTOCOPIES

I authorize that photocopies of this instrument may be made, and that these photocopies shall have the same force and effect as the original.

EFFECTIVE DATE

This instrument shall become effectively immediately, and it shall not be affected by my subsequent disability or incapacity.

_____   Signed on _____, 20_____.
(STUDENT NAME)

NOTORIZATION

STATE OF _____; COUNTY OF _____, I, undersigned, a Notary Public in and for the jurisdiction aforesaid, in the state of _____, do hereby certify that _(STUDENT NAME),_ whose name is signed to the foregoing Specific Power of Attorney for Educational Decisions, has acknowledged the same before me in the jurisdiction aforesaid. Given under my hand this:_____ day of _____, 20_____.

_____ (Notary Public) My Commission Expires _____

ATTORNEY'S CERTIFICATION

I am a lawyer authorized to practice law in Georgia. I have advised my client concerning the rights in connection with this Specific Power of Attorney for Educational Decisions.

_____
(NAME OF ATTORNEY).

This document was drafted by:
(NAME OF ATTORNEY); (GA BAR NO)
(ATTORNEY ADDRESS); (ATTORNEY PHONE/EMAIL)

NOTE: This document, with original signatures, must be filed with the student's school record before an Agent can be recognized. For the _(NAME OF SCHOOL)_ to recognize any changes or revocations, written notification to _(NAME OF SCHOOL)_ must be provided those changes or revocation. Such notification must be dated and witnessed. _(Alternative to POA is a supported decision making agreement_ _http://www.supporteddecisionmaking.org/sites/default/files/sample-supported-decision-making-model-agreements.pdf)_

STATE OF _____

COUNTY OF _____

PARENT/GUARDIAN NAME	]
Address	]
City-State-Zip	]
Ph.	]
Email	]
Parent/Legal Guardian	]
	]
	] STUDENT NAME
To	] DOB-00/00/0000
	]
NAME OF SCHOOL SYSTEM	]
Special Education Director Name	]
School System Address	]
School City-State-Zip	]
Respondent	]
	]

NOTICE OF STAY PUT UNDER THE INDIVIDUALS WITH DISABILITIES EDUCATION ACT

Be advised that NAME OF STUDENT, will remain in his/her current placement in accordance with 34 C.F.R. § 300.518(a) that states:

Except as provided in § 300.533, during the pendency of any administrative or judicial proceeding regarding a due process complaint notice requesting a due process hearing under $300.507, unless the State or local agency *and* the parents of the child agree otherwise, the child involved in the complaint MUST remain in his or her current educational placement.

In accordance with the above, a request for a due process hearing will be filed within the next 10 days.

_____

Parent/Legal Guardian of Above Named Student   Date

SUPPORTED DECISION-MAKING AGREEMENT

My Name is: _____ Today's Date is:_____

I want to have people I trust to help me make decisions. The people who will help me are called supporters. I can say what kind of help my supporters will give me. If I want supporters to help me make choices about money, I will sign a different agreement, called "Supported Decision-Making Agreement for Finances."

SUPPORTER:

Name: _____ Address: _____

Phone No: _____ Email: _____

I want this person to help me with:
      Making Choices about My Education

My supporters are NOT allowed to make choices for me. To help me with my choices, my supporters may:

      Help me find out more about my choices; help me understand my choices so I can make a good decision for myself; and help me tell other people about my decision

I am including the following forms to this agreement:
Request for Production of Documents & Authorization for Release of Confidential Information to a Third Party

This supported decision-making agreement starts right now and will continue until the agreement is stopped by me or my supporters.

Signature of Adult with a Disability

My Signature:_____ My Printed Name:_____

My Address:_____ My Phone Number:_____

My Email Address: _____

Consent of Supporters

I, _____ consent to act as _____'s supporter under this agreement. I understand that my job as a supporter is to honor and express his/her wishes. My support might include giving this person information in a way he/she can understand; discussing pros and cons of decisions; and helping this person communicate his/her choice. I know that I may NOT make decisions for this person. I agree to support this person's decision to the best of my ability, honestly, and in good faith.

_____

Signature of Supporter   Date

The Education Commission of the States (ECS) tracks state policies on suspension and expulsion limitations across all 50 states. Many states have placed restrictions on when, how, and for how long a student can be suspended or expelled. These limitations generally focus on the following key areas:

1. Grade-Level and Age Restrictions

- Preschool & Early Grades: Many states now limit or prohibit suspensions and expulsions for young students (e.g., K-2 or K-3), except in cases of violent behavior or weapons.
- Elementary vs. Secondary: Some states impose shorter suspension limits for younger students and stricter due process protections before expelling them.

2. Suspension Duration Limits

- Many states set maximum suspension periods, often 10 days or less for short-term suspensions.
- Long-term suspensions (over 10 days) require additional hearings or board approvals in many states.

3. Expulsion Limitations

- Some states prohibit expulsions for non-violent or minor infractions (e.g., dress code violations, minor disruptive behavior).
- Certain states require alternative education placements for expelled students.

4. Due Process Protections

- Hearings & Appeals: Some states require disciplinary hearings before a long-term suspension or expulsion can be enforced.
- Parental Notification: Schools must provide written notice to parents and offer an appeal process in many states.

5. Limits on Suspensions for Subjective Offenses

- Some states prohibit suspensions for "willful defiance" or other vague disciplinary reasons, particularly in early grades.

The appendix of this book contains a chart of all 50 states laws on suspension/expulsion but you are encouraged to verify this information with your state's educational authority as laws change frequently.

STATE OF GEORGIA
COUNTY OF _____

PARENT NAME]
Parent/Student Address]
Parent City/State/Zip]
Parent Phone]
Parent Email Address]
    Parent/Legal Guardian]

]   STUDENT NAME
To]   STUDENT DOB
SCHOOL DISTRICT NAME]
School Address]
School City/State/Zip]
School Phone]
School Email]
    Respondent]

NOTICE OF OCGA 20-2-742-MULTI-TIERED SYSTEM OF SUPPORTS PRIOR TO SUSPENSION OR EXPULSION FOR CERTAIN STUDENTS (PRE-K THROUGH 3RD GRADE)

(a)As used in this Code section, the term:

    (1) Multi-tiered system of supports" or "MTSS" means a systemic, continuous-improvement framework in which data based problem solving and decision making is practiced across all levels of the educational system for supporting students at multiple levels of intervention.

    (2) "Public preschool through third grade" means a public preschool, a Pre-K program in a public school administered pursuant to Code Section 20-1A-4, and kindergarten through third grade in a public school.

    (3) "Response to intervention" or "RTI" means a framework of identifying and addressing the academic and behavioral needs of students through a tiered system.

    (4) "Weapon" shall include dangerous weapons, firearms, and hazardous objects as defined in Code Section 20-2-751.

(b)No student in public preschool through third grade shall be expelled or suspended from school for more than five consecutive or cumulative days during a school year without first receiving a multi-tiered system of supports, such as response to intervention, unless such student possessed a weapon, illegal drugs, or other dangerous instrument or such student's behavior endangers the physical safety of other students or school personnel. If such student is receiving or has received a multi-tiered system of supports, the school shall be deemed to have met the requirements of this Code section. The school or program shall comply with all federal laws and requirements regarding obtaining parental consent during any advanced tier within the system of supports prior to certain screenings or evaluations.

(c)In addition to the requirements in subsection (b) of this Code section, prior to assigning any student in preschool through third grade to out-of-school suspension for more than five consecutive or cumulative days during a school year, if such student has an Individualized Education Program (IEP) pursuant to the federal Individuals with Disabilities Education Act or a plan under Section 504 of the federal Rehabilitation Act of 1973, the school or program shall also convene an IEP or Section 504 meeting to review appropriate supports being provided as part of such Individualized Education Program or Section 504 plan.

Should the respondent violate this law, parent will have no alternative but to file a complaints.

_____   _____
PARENT SIGNATURE   DATE

<u>TEACHER INTRODUCTION TO STUDENT LETTER</u>

PARENT NAME
PARENT ADDRESS
PARENT PHONE/EMAIL

DATE

Re: STUDENT NAME
         DOB: STUDENT DOB

Dear Educator,

We are writing this letter to introduce you to our child and to thank you in advance for your support. Since you will be spending more time with *STUDENT NAME* than with your own family during the week, we want you to know that we appreciate the sacrifices you are making daily to teach them. We want your candid feedback even though it may not always be easy for us to hear and we value your enthusiasm for teaching especially at times when they may not be motivated to do their best. *STUDENT NAME* needs our help not just academically but to also become a productive member of society.

Please find enclosed a copy of the most recent evaluation. Also enclosed is the most recent IEP and a *(MOVIE/BROCHURE)* about *(NAME OF DISABILITY)*. *(STUDENT NAME)* has *(NAME OF DISABILITY)* which is on the mild end of the autism spectrum. *You will notice that (STUDENT NAME) is sensitive to loud noises and sensations and he is a very picky eater. You will also notice these features in the movie as well and we hope you enjoy it!*

As for *(STUDENT NAME)*, *he is a member of Boy Scout Troop 32 and he participated in camp with Boy Scouts and went on a Carnival Cruise to the Bahamas over the summer. He has a very strong interest in WWII or anything military for that matter.* If you have any questions about our child or need anything for your classroom in the way of supplies let us know. We are happy to help. Let's make this a great year!

Sincerely,
(PARENT/GUARDIAN NAME)

(Customize italics portion for your child)
For disability movies (https://iris.peabody.vanderbilt.edu/resources/films/)

A 10-day withdrawal letter in special education is a formal notice a parent or guardian gives to a school district stating their intent to withdraw their child from the public school system, typically to:

1. Unilaterally place the child in a private school, and
2. Seek reimbursement for the cost of that private placement.

Why 10 Days?

Under the Individuals with Disabilities Education Act (IDEA), parents are required to notify the school district at least 10 business days prior to removing their child from public school if they intend to:

- Place the child in a private school due to disagreements with the IEP or FAPE (Free Appropriate Public Education) provided by the district, and
- Later seek reimbursement from the district for the private school tuition.

What the Letter Typically Includes:

- The date of intended withdrawal
- The reasons the parent believes the school failed to provide FAPE
- The name and address of the intended private school, if known
- A statement that the parent intends to seek reimbursement

Purpose:

- Gives the school district an opportunity to address the concerns and potentially correct the IEP or placement
- Helps courts and hearing officers assess whether the parent's actions were reasonable
- Can affect the amount of tuition reimbursement awarded, if any

STATE OF_____
COUNTY OF _____

PARENT NAME	]
Parent/Student Address	]
Parent City/State/Zip	]
Parent Phone	]
Parent Email Address	]
Parent/Legal Guardian	]
	] STUDENT NAME
To	] STUDENT DOB
SCHOOL DISTRICT NAME	]
School Address	]
School City/State/Zip	]
School Phone	]
School Email	]
Respondent	]

TEN (10) DAY NOTICE OF UNILATERAL PLACEMENT

I am writing to formally notify you, pursuant to the Individuals with Disabilities Education Act (IDEA), of my intent to withdraw my child, [Child's Name], from [School Name], effective [Insert Date, at least 10 business days from today].

I have serious concerns that the current IEP and educational placement being provided by the district fails to offer my child a Free Appropriate Public Education (FAPE). Specifically, [briefly list reasons, e.g., "the district has not provided appropriate speech-language services," or "my child's behavioral needs are not being adequately addressed."]

As a result, I intend to place [Child's Name] at [Private School Name, if known], which I believe can meet my child's educational needs. I also intend to seek reimbursement from the school district for the cost of this private placement.

Please let me know if the district is willing to reconvene the IEP team or propose an appropriate resolution before the withdrawal date.

Sincerely,

_____

Parent/Guardian   Date

TRUANCY CRIMES COMMITTED BY SCHOOLS LETTER

(PARENT/GUARDIAN NAME)
(Parent/Guardian Address)
(Parent Guardian phone/email)

(Date)

(School Name)
(School Address)
(School City, State, Zip)

Re: (Student Name)
        (Student DOB **/**/****)

As of this date, (Student Name) has already excessive days of school due to directives requiring (him/her) to be removed from the academic setting. This is primarily due to documented and undocumented suspensions that resulted from ineffective behavioral interventions. This pattern demonstrates that (Name of School) has not fully provided (Student Name) with a Free Appropriate Public Education (FAPE) and raises serious concerns about its ability to do so moving forward.

It is (my/our) position that (Name of School)'s actions contribute to educational deprivation and potentially violate truancy laws designed to ensure students remain in school. It appears that governmental immunity is being used not only as a shield against accountability but also as a means to deny (Student Name) access to the education and supports to which (he/she) is legally entitled. To ensure transparency and compliance, (I/we) will notify law enforcement should (Student Name) be directed to leave the academic setting again. The goal is not confrontation, but rather to encourage staff to prioritize keeping (Student Name) in school and providing the appropriate supports that (Name of School) has thus far failed to implement.

That said, should this situation persist, (I/we) will have no alternative but to file ethics complaints regarding teaching credentials, using documentation collected through the appropriate legal channels. It is (my/our) sincere hope that such measures will not be necessary, as our shared focus should be on ensuring (Student Name) receives the education (he/she) deserves.

Truancy laws exist to keep students in school, and it is deeply concerning when an institution meant to foster learning instead creates barriers to access. Schools should be promoting attendance, not enforcing policies that undermine a child's right to education. Nonetheless, (I/we) remain hopeful that at the upcoming (Individualized Education Program (IEP)) meeting that we are now requesting, we can work collaboratively to develop a plan that supports (Student Name)'s success while ensuring compliance with the law and best educational practices.

Sincerely,
(Name of Parent)

Cc: Local Superintendent/BOE Members; Local Law Enforcement; Child Protective Services; State Senator/Rep

STATE OF _____
COUNTY OF _____

Parent/Student Name
Parent/Student Address
P/S, City/State/Zip
   Parent/Legal Guardian

                            STUDENT NAME
          To   STUDENT DOB

School Name
School Address
School City/State/Zip
   Respondent

NOTICE OF REQUIRED ACCOMMODATIONS

This is to inform you that, pursuant to rights as stated under the Americans with Disabilities Act, the following accommodations are needed for full access to the scheduled Individualized Education Meeting scheduled for (DATE OF MEETING):

INTERPRETER (for example)
-(ACCOMMODATION 2)
-(ACCOMMODATION 3)

20 USC 12182:

    No individual shall be discriminated against on the basis of disability in the full and equal enjoyment of the goods, services, facilities, privileges, advantages, or accommodations of any place of public accommodation by any person who owns, leases (or leases to), or operates a place of public accommodation

Please confirm with me on or before (DATE) whether the above accommodations will be available for the meeting so that I can am able to fully and equally participate.

Respectfully Submitted,
PARENT NAME

REQUEST FOR PRESERVATION AND PRODUCTION FOR VIDEO

A Request for Preservation and Production of Video is typically made in legal proceedings when video footage may contain evidence that is relevant and material to the case. Here's a breakdown of why you would make this request:

1. To Prevent Destruction or Loss of Evidence

Video surveillance or recordings are often kept for only a limited time before being automatically deleted or overwritten. Making a formal request to preserve the footage helps ensure it isn't lost.

2. Because the Video May Be Key Evidence

You would request the production of video when it might:

- Show what actually happened during an incident (e.g., a fight, arrest, injury, school misconduct).
- Corroborate or contradict witness testimony.
- Reveal procedural errors, discrimination, or abuse.

3. To Support or Refute Claims

If you're representing a client (such as a student in a school discipline case), video can:

- Show whether they actually did what they're accused of.
- Provide context—was the student provoked? Was the punishment disproportionate?
- Show bias or inconsistent treatment compared to other students.

4. To Create a Record of Your Request

Formally requesting preservation creates a paper trail. If the video is destroyed after your request, you may be able to argue spoliation of evidence, which can lead to legal consequences for the other side (such as sanctions or inferences in your favor).

Example Scenario

Let's say a student is accused of assaulting another student in a school hallway. There's a surveillance camera that points to the hallway. As the student's attorney, you'd request preservation and production of that video to:

- See what really happened.
- Determine if staff intervened appropriately.
- Use it to defend the student or negotiate a better outcome.

STATE OF _____
COUNTY OF _____

Parent/Student Name	]
Parent/Student Address	]
P/S, City/State/Zip	]
Phone #	]
Email Address	]
Parent/Legal Guardian	]
	] STUDENT NAME
To	] STUDENT DOB
Principal	]
School Name	]
School Address	]
School City/State/Zip	]
Respondent	]

REQUEST FOR PRESERVATION AND PRODUCTION OF VIDEO

I am the PARENT/GUARDIAN of STUDENT NAME, who is a student enrolled and attending NAME OF SCHOOL. I am writing to report an incident involving STUDENT NAME in the education classroom. The classroom is under video and audio surveillance pursuant to state open records act. Therefore, I am writing to demand the release of video and audio recordings of the incident for viewing by me as authorized pursuant to state open records act. My child's education placement is:

CLASSROOM/SETTING ROOM NUMBER

CLASSROOM/SETTING TEACHER

To the best of my knowledge at this time, I have the following information on the incident involving my child.

Dates of alleged incident(s):

SPECIFIC DATES OR REASONABLE DATE RANGE, SUCH AS A PARTICULAR WEEK

Time(s) of alleged incident(s):

SPECIFIC TIME OR PERIOD OF DAY, SUCH AS MORNING OR END OF SCHOOL DAY

Description of alleged incident(s):

DESCRIBE ABUSE OR NEGLECT, SUCH AS PHYSICAL INJURY BY A STAFF MEMBER OR SEXUAL ABUSE BY ANOTHER STUDENT

Identification of witness(es):

NAMES OF INDIVIDUALS THAT YOU ARE AWARE OF WHO OBSERVED FIRST-HAND THE INCIDENT(S), SUCH AS A TEACHER, AIDE, OR ANOTHER STUDENT

If the school has already made a report Child Protective Services about the incident, then I ask that you please inform me.

Please contact me as soon as possible to arrange the location and time for release of for viewing the requested recordings. If the district denies my request, then please send me the denial in writing along with a copy of the local internal grievance policy. Under state law, I request that the district maintain, preserve, and save all video and audio recordings of STUDENT NAME education classroom beyond the mandatory minimum period until all investigations, determinations, and appeals have been fully completed.

Sincerely,
SIGNATURE
NAME
ADDRESS
CITY, STATE, ZIP
PHONE NUMBER
EMAIL ADDRESS

Cc: District Superintendent

APPENDIX

DEPARTMENT OF EDUCATION WEBSITES FOR ALL 50 STATES

Alabama	https://www.alabamaachieves.org/
Alaska	https://education.alaska.gov/
Arizona	https://www.azed.gov/
Arkansas	https://dese.ade.arkansas.gov/
California	https://www.cde.ca.gov/
Colorado	https://www.cde.state.co.us/
Connecticut	https://portal.ct.gov/sde
Delaware	https://education.delaware.gov/
Florida	https://www.fldoe.org/
Georgia	https://gadoe.org/
Hawaii	https://hawaiipublicschools.org/
Idaho	https://www.sde.idaho.gov/
Illinois	https://www.isbe.net/
Indiana	https://www.in.gov/doe/
Iowa	https://educate.iowa.gov/
Kansas	https://www.ksde.gov/
Kentucky	https://www.education.ky.gov/Pages/default.aspx
Louisiana	https://doe.louisiana.gov/
Maine	https://www.maine.gov/doe/
Maryland	https://marylandpublicschools.org/Pages/Default.aspx
Massachusetts	https://www.doe.mass.edu/
Michigan	https://www.michigan.gov/mde
Mississippi	https://mdek12.org/
Missouri	https://dese.mo.gov/
Montana	https://opi.mt.gov/
Nebraska	https://www.education.ne.gov/
Nevada	https://doe.nv.gov/
New Hampshire	https://www.education.nh.gov/
New Jersey	https://www.nj.gov/education/
New Mexico	https://webnew.ped.state.nm.us/
New York	https://www.nysed.gov/
North Carolina	https://www.dpi.nc.gov/
North Dakota	https://www.nd.gov/dpi/
Ohio	https://education.ohio.gov/
Oklahoma	https://oklahoma.gov/education.html
Oregon	https://www.oregon.gov/ode/Pages/default.aspx
Pennsylvania	https://www.pa.gov/agencies/education.html
Rhode Island	https://ride.ri.gov/
South Carolina	https://ed.sc.gov/
South Dakota	https://doe.sd.gov/
Tennessee	https://www.tn.gov/education.html
Texas	https://tea.texas.gov/
Utah	https://www.schools.utah.gov/
Vermont	https://education.vermont.gov/
Virginia	https://www.doe.virginia.gov/
Washington	https://ospi.k12.wa.us/
West Virginia	https://wvde.us/
Wisconsin	https://dpi.wi.gov/
Wyoming	https://edu.wyoming.gov/

EDUCATOR CREDENTIALING ENTITIES FOR ALL 50 STATES

State	Organization	Website
Alabama	Alabama State Department of Education – Educator Certification	https://www.alabamaachieves.org
Alaska	Alaska Department of Education & Early Development – Teacher Certification	https://education.alaska.gov
Arizona	Arizona Department of Education – Certification Unit	https://www.azed.gov
Arkansas	Arkansas Department of Education – Educator Licensure	https://dese.ade.arkansas.gov
California	California Commission on Teacher Credentialing (CTC)	https://www.ctc.ca.gov
Colorado	Colorado Department of Education – Educator Licensing	https://www.cde.state.co.us
Connecticut	Connecticut State Department of Education – Bureau of Educator Standards and Certification	https://portal.ct.gov/SDE
Delaware	Delaware Department of Education – Educator Credentialing	https://www.doe.k12.de.us
Florida	Florida Department of Education – Educator Certification	https://www.fldoe.org
Georgia	Georgia Professional Standards Commission	https://www.gapsc.com
Hawaii	Hawaii Teacher Standards Board	https://hawaiiteacherstandardsboard.org
Idaho	Idaho State Department of Education – Certification & Professional Standards	https://www.sde.idaho.gov
Illinois	Illinois State Board of Education – Educator Licensure	https://www.isbe.net
Indiana	Indiana Department of Education – Office of Educator Licensing	https://www.in.gov/doe
Iowa	Iowa Board of Educational Examiners	https://www.boee.iowa.gov
Kansas	Kansas State Department of Education – Teacher Licensure	https://www.ksde.org
Kentucky	Kentucky Education Professional Standards Board	https://www.epsb.ky.gov
Louisiana	Louisiana Department of Education – Educator Certification	https://www.louisianabelieves.com
Maine	Maine Department of Education – Certification Office	https://www.maine.gov/doe
Maryland	Maryland State Department of Education – Certification Branch	https://www.marylandpublicschools.org
Massachusetts	Massachusetts Department of Elementary & Secondary Education – Licensure Office	https://www.doe.mass.edu
Michigan	Michigan Department of Education – Office of Educator Excellence	https://www.michigan.gov/mde
Minnesota	Minnesota Professional Educator Licensing and Standards Board	https://mn.gov/pelsb
Mississippi	Mississippi Department of Education – Office of Educator Licensure	https://www.mdek12.org
Missouri	Missouri Department of Elementary & Secondary Education – Educator Certification	https://dese.mo.gov

Montana	Montana Office of Public Instruction – Educator Licensure	https://opi.mt.gov
Nebraska	Nebraska Department of Education – Educator Certification	https://www.education.ne.gov
Nevada	Nevada Department of Education – Educator Licensure	https://doe.nv.gov
New Hampshire	New Hampshire Department of Education – Bureau of Credentialing	https://www.education.nh.gov
New Jersey	New Jersey Department of Education – Office of Certification and Induction	https://www.nj.gov/education
New Mexico	New Mexico Public Education Department – Educator Licensure	https://webnew.ped.state.nm.us
New York	New York State Education Department – Office of Teaching Initiatives	https://www.highered.nysed.gov/tcert
North Carolina	North Carolina Department of Public Instruction – Licensure	https://www.dpi.nc.gov
North Dakota	North Dakota Education Standards and Practices Board	https://www.nd.gov/espb
Ohio	Ohio Department of Education – Educator Licensure	https://education.ohio.gov
Oklahoma	Oklahoma State Department of Education – Teacher Certification	https://sde.ok.gov
Oregon	Oregon Teacher Standards and Practices Commission	https://www.oregon.gov/tspc
Pennsylvania	Pennsylvania Department of Education – Certification Services	https://www.education.pa.gov
Rhode Island	Rhode Island Department of Education – Educator Certification	https://www.ride.ri.gov
South Carolina	South Carolina Department of Education – Educator Certification	https://ed.sc.gov
South Dakota	South Dakota Department of Education – Educator Certification	https://doe.sd.gov
Tennessee	Tennessee Department of Education – Educator Licensure	https://www.tn.gov/education
Texas	Texas Education Agency – Educator Certification	https://tea.texas.gov
Utah	Utah State Board of Education – Educator Licensing	https://www.schools.utah.gov
Vermont	Vermont Agency of Education – Educator Licensing	https://education.vermont.gov
Virginia	Virginia Department of Education – Licensure	https://www.doe.virginia.gov
Washington	Washington State Professional Educator Standards Board	https://www.pesb.wa.gov
West Virginia	West Virginia Department of Education – Office of Certification	https://wvde.us
Wisconsin	Wisconsin Department of Public Instruction – Educator Licensing	https://dpi.wi.gov
Wyoming	Wyoming Professional Teaching Standards Board	https://wyomingptsb.com

SUSPENSION/EXPULSION LAW: 50 STATES

Alabama	N/A
Alaska	N/A
Arizona	§ 15-841
Arkansas	§ 6-18-507
California	§ 48900; §48903; §352; §353
Colorado	§ 22-33-105
Connecticut	§ 10-233a; §10-233c; § 10-233f
Delaware	§ 8104; Reg. 14616
District of Columbia	§2408; § 2502; § 2504; §38-273.03; B22-0594
Florida	§ 1006.09
Georgia	§20-2-742
Hawaii	Reg. 8-19-6
Idaho	§33-205
Illinois	5/10-22.6; 5/26-12
Indiana	§20-33-8-18; §20-33-8-20
Iowa	N/A
Kansas	§74-6132; §72-6115
Kentucky	§158.150
Louisiana	17.416
Maine	20-A § 1001
Maryland	§7-305; §7-305.1
Massachusetts	71§84
Michigan	§380.1301; §380.1310; §380.1311a; §388.1767a
Minnesota	§121A41; §121A61
Mississippi	N/A
Missouri	§167.161
Montana	§20-5-202
Nebraska	§79-267; §79-283; §28-1204.04
Nevada	§392.466; §392.467; §392.4634; §392.4657
New Hampshire	§193.13
New Jersey	§18A37-2a
New Mexico	§22-12-9; 6.11.2.7

New York	§3214
North Carolina	§115C-390.1; §115C-390.10; §115C-390.2
North Dakota	§15.1-19-09
Ohio	§3313.66; §3313.668; HB318
Oklahoma	70,§24-101.3
Oregon	§339.250
Pennsylvania	§13-1317.2
Rhode Island	§16-19-1; §16-21-21.1; §11-47-60.2
South Carolina	§59-150-250
South Dakota	N/A
Tennessee	§49-6-3401
Texas	§37.005; §37.001
Utah	§53G-8-206
Vermont	16, §1162
Virginia	§22.1.277; §22.1.277.04; §22.1.277.05
Washington	§28A.600.015; §28A.600.420; §28A.600.020; 392-400-245
West Virginia	§18A-5-1a; §18A-5-1
Wisconsin	§120.13
Wyoming	§21-4-305

OPEN RECORDS/SIMILAR LAWS: 50 STATES

Alabama	§ 36-25A-1	Virginia	§ 2.2-3700 – 2.2-3714
Alaska	§ 09.25.110	Washington	Chapter 42.56 RCW
Arizona	§ 39-121	West Virginia	W.Va. Code §29B-1-1
Arkansas	§25-19-101	Wisconsin	Wisconsin Statute 19.21
California	§6250-6268	Wyoming	Wyo. Stat. § 16-4-201
Colorado	C.R.S. 24-72-201		
Connecticut	Connecticut FOIA		
District of Columbia	D.C. Code § 2-531-540		
Delaware	Title 29, Chapter 100		
Florida	Fla. Stat. sec. 119.01		
Georgia	O.C.G.A. §50-18-70		
Hawaii	Haw. Rev. Stat. §91-1		
Idaho	Idaho Code §74-101		
Illinois	Illinois FOIA		
Indiana	§5-14-3-1		
Iowa	§22.1		
Kansas	KSA 45-215		
Kentucky	61.870		
Louisiana	La.R.S. 44:1		
Maine	Title 1, Chapter 13		
Maryland	§ 4-101		
Massachusetts	G. L. c. 4, § 7(26)		
Michigan	Mich. Comp. Laws Ann.§15.231		
Minnesota	Minn. Statutes 13.01		
Mississippi	Miss. Code Ann. 25-61-1		
Missouri	Mo. Code §610.023		
Montana	Montana Code 2-6-101		
Nebraska	§84-712.01		
Nevada	N.R.S. 239 et seq.		
New Hampshire	R.S.A. Ch. 91-A		
New Jersey	P.L.1963, c. 73		
New Mexico	NMSA (1978) 14-2		
New York	New York FOIL		
North Carolina	Section § 132-6		
North Dakota	NDCC 44-04-18		
Ohio	Ohio Rev. Code sec. 149.43		
Oklahoma	Title 51 OK Statutes § 24A.1		
Oregon	O.R.S. 192.410		
Pennsylvania	65 PA Statute § 67.101		
Rhode Island	R.I. Gen. Laws §38-2-1		
South Carolina	§30-4-10 to 30-4-55		
South Dakota	SDCL Chapter 1-27		
Tennessee	CodeAnn. 10-7-503		
Texas	TX Gvmnt Code 552		
Utah	Title 63G Chapter 2		
Vermont	Title 1, Chapter 5.315	ALL STATES	https://www.nfoic.org/state-freedom-of-information-laws/

RECORDING CONVERSATIONS: 50 STATE CONSENT LAWS

ONE PARTY	CONSENT STATES	TWO PARTY	CONSENT STATES
Alabama	Ala. Code § 13A-11-30	California	Cal. Penal Code § 632
Alaska	Alaska Stat. § 42.20.310	Connecticut	Conn. Gen. Stat. § 52-570d
Arizona	Ariz. Rev. Stat. Ann. § 13-3005	Delaware	Del. Code Ann. tit. 11, § 1335
Arkansas	Ark. Code Ann. § 5-60-120	Florida	Fla. Stat. § 934.03
Colorado	Colo. Rev. Stat. § 18-9-303	Illinois	720 Ill. Comp. Stat. 5/14-2
District of Columbia	D.C. Code § 23-542	Maryland	Md. Code Ann., Cts. & Jud. Proc. § 10-402
Georgia	O.C.G.A. § 16-11-66	Massachusetts	Mass. Gen. Laws ch. 272, § 99
Hawaii (*one party for calls; varies in-person*)	Haw. Rev. Stat. § 803-42(b)(3)	Michigan (*law says one-party; courts differ*)	Mich. Comp. Laws § 750.539c
Idaho	Idaho Code Ann. § 18-6702	Montana	Mont. Code Ann. § 45-8-213
Indiana	Ind. Code Ann. § 35-33.5-1-5	Nevada	Nev. Rev. Stat. Ann. § 200.620
Iowa	Iowa Code Ann. § 808B.2	New Hampshire	N.H. Rev. Stat. Ann. § 570-A:2
Kansas	Kan. Stat. Ann. § 21-6101	Pennsylvania	18 Pa.C.S.A. § 5703
Kentucky	Ky. Rev. Stat. Ann. § 526.010	Washington	RCW 9.73.030
Lousiana	La. Rev. Stat. Ann. § 15:1303		
Maine (*one-party for calls; see notes*)	Me. Rev. Stat. Ann. tit. 15, § 710		
Minnesota	Minn. Stat. Ann. § 626A.02		
Mississippi	Miss. Code Ann. § 41-29-531		
Missouri	Mo. Ann. Stat. § 542.402		
Nebraska	Neb. Rev. Stat. § 86-290		
New Jersey	N.J. Stat. Ann. § 2A:156A-4		
New Mexico	N.M. Stat. Ann. § 30-12-1		
New York	N.Y. Penal Law §§ 250.00, 250.05		
North Carolina	N.C. Gen. Stat. § 15A-287		
North Dakota	N.D. Cent. Code § 12.1-15-02		
Ohio	Ohio Rev. Code Ann. § 2933.52		
Oklahoma	Okla. Stat. Ann. tit. 13, § 176.4		
Oregon (*one-party for calls; all-party for in person*)	Or. Rev. Stat. § 165.540		
Rhode Island	R.I. Gen. Laws § 11-35-21		
South Carolina	S.C. Code Ann. § 17-30-30		
South Dakota	S.D. Codified Laws § 23A-35A-20		
Tennessee	Tenn. Code Ann. § 39-13-601		
Texas	Tex. Penal Code Ann. § 16.02		
Utah	Utah Code Ann. § 77-23a-4		
Vermont	(*no law; follows federal one-party rule*)		
Virginia	Va. Code Ann. § 19.2-62		
West Virginia	W. Va. Code § 62-1D-3		
Wisconsin	Wis. Stat. Ann. § 968.31		
Wyoming	Wyo. Stat. Ann. § 7-3-702		

Hawaii: Requires two-party consent for some in-person recordings.

Maine: In-person recording may require consent under privacy law.

Michigan: Statute says one-party, but courts are divided.

Oregon: One-party consent for phone calls; all-party for in-person.

Vermont: No statute—follows federal one-party consent standard.

A

Academic – Related to education, scholarship, or learning.

Accessible Educational Materials (AEM) – Learning materials that are usable by students with print disabilities (e.g., Braille, audiobooks, large print).

Accessible Instructional Materials (AIM) – Learning materials made available in formats that are accessible to students with disabilities.

Accommodation – Supports provided to help students access the curriculum.

Accreditation – Official recognition that an institution meets certain standards.

Accommodations – Changes in how a student accesses information or demonstrates learning (e.g., extended time, quiet setting).

Achievement – The measurable performance or progress of a student.

Acquisition – The process of learning or gaining new knowledge or skills (e.g., language acquisition).

Adaptations – Modifications to curriculum or instruction to meet a student's individual needs.

Administrator – A person responsible for managing a school or educational program.

Advocacy – Supporting or speaking up for student needs and rights.

Advocate – A person (often a parent, attorney, or trained professional) who supports and defends the rights of a student with disabilities.

Aide (or Paraprofessional) – A support staff member who assists students with disabilities under the direction of a certified teacher.

Alignment – Ensuring curriculum, instruction, and assessment are connected and support learning goals.

Alternate Assessment – An assessment designed for students with significant cognitive disabilities who are unable to participate in general assessments, even with accommodations.

Alternative Education – Non-traditional education settings for students with diverse needs.

Annual Goals – Specific, measurable objectives in a student's IEP designed to be achieved within one year.

Annual Review – A required yearly meeting to assess and update a student's IEP.

Applied Behavior Analysis (ABA) – A therapy based on behaviorist theories often used with students with autism.

Apprenticeship – A training system that combines on-the-job experience with classroom instruction.

Articulation – Coordination between educational institutions to ensure smooth student transitions.

Assessment – Tools and methods used to evaluate a student's abilities, strengths, and needs; includes both formal (standardized) and informal measures.

Assistive Technology (AT) – Devices or software that help students with disabilities learn and communicate (e.g., speech-to-text tools).

Asynchronous Learning – Learning that doesn't occur in the same place or at the same time.

Attendance – The act of being present at school or class.

Autism Spectrum Disorder (ASD) – A developmental disability affecting communication, behavior, and social interaction.

B

Baseline Data-The initial data collected on a student's performance before interventions begin; used to measure progress.

Basic Skills-Foundational academic or functional skills such as reading, writing, math, and social interaction.

Behavioral Goals-Specific targets related to improving behavior, often part of an IEP or BIP.

Behavior Intervention Plan (BIP)-A formal plan used to address challenging behavior in students, based on a Functional Behavior Assessment (FBA).

Behavior Support Strategies and interventions used to help students develop positive behaviors and reduce problematic ones.

Benchmarks-Short-term objectives or steps toward achieving a long-term IEP goal.

Bilingual Special Education-Services that address both the language and special education needs of students who are English learners.

Board Certified Behavior Analyst (BCBA)-A professional certified to design and implement behavior intervention plans and conduct assessments.

Braille-A tactile writing system used by individuals who are visually impaired.

Built Environment-Physical surroundings in a school setting that should be accessible to all students, including those with disabilities.

Bullying Prevention-Programs or strategies designed to prevent bullying, which disproportionately affects students with disabilities.

Bypass Strategies-Techniques that allow a student to work around a disability (e.g., using speech-to-text software for a student with dysgraphia).

C

Child Find-A legal requirement under IDEA that schools identify, locate, and evaluate all children with disabilities who may need special education services.

Case Manager-A professional (often a special education teacher) responsible for overseeing a student's IEP and coordinating services.

Curriculum-Based Assessment (CBA)-A method of evaluating a student's academic performance using the curriculum they are being taught.

Classroom Accommodations-Adjustments to teaching methods, materials, or the classroom environment to help a student access learning (e.g., extra time on tests, preferential seating).

Consent (Informed Consent)-A parent or guardian's written agreement for evaluation or services, given after being fully informed of the procedures and implications.

Cognitive Disability-A disability that affects intellectual functioning and adaptive behavior, potentially impacting learning and daily living.

Collaborative Teaching (Co-Teaching)-A model where a general education and special education teacher work together to instruct all students in an inclusive classroom.

Compensatory Education-Educational services ordered to make up for services that were not provided as required by a student's IEP.

Counseling Services-A related service under IDEA that supports students' emotional, social, or behavioral needs.

Continuum of Services-A range of placement options (from general education to self-contained classes) to meet the needs of students with disabilities.

Corrective Feedback-Immediate feedback provided to students to help them understand and correct their errors.

Communication DisorderA disability that affects a student's ability to understand, process, or express language.

Closed Captioning-A text display of spoken dialogue and sounds, helpful for students who are deaf or hard of hearing.

Check-In/Check-Out (CICO)-A behavior intervention strategy where students check in with an adult at the beginning and end of the day to reinforce positive behavior.

D

Data Collection-The systematic gathering of information to monitor student progress, evaluate interventions, or inform decisions in IEP development.

Deaf-Blindness-A dual sensory impairment that significantly affects communication, development, and educational needs.

Desensitization-A behavioral technique that gradually reduces fear or anxiety related to a specific situation or stimulus.

Designated Instruction and Services (DIS)-A California-specific term for related services (like speech therapy, counseling) provided to support a student's IEP goals.

Developmental Delay-A term used for children ages 3–9 who show delays in physical, cognitive, communication, social/emotional, or adaptive development.

Developmental Disability-A chronic condition that originates before age 22 and causes substantial limitations in multiple life areas, such as learning, mobility, or self-care.

Diagnostic Assessment-An evaluation that identifies a student's strengths and weaknesses in specific areas to guide instruction and interventions.

Diagnostic and Statistical Manual of Mental Disorders (DSM)-A manual used by clinicians to diagnose mental health conditions; often referenced in identifying qualifying disabilities under IDEA.

Differentiated Instruction-Tailoring instruction to meet individual students' needs, including varying content, process, products, or learning environment.

Direct Instruction-A structured, teacher-led approach that uses clear, explicit teaching of skills, often used in special education settings.

Disability-A physical, mental, emotional, or developmental condition that substantially limits one or more major life activities, and may qualify a student for special education services under IDEA or Section 504.

Disproportionality-The over- or under-representation of a particular demographic group (e.g., race or ethnicity) in special education or specific disability categories.

Dropout Prevention-Programs or strategies aimed at keeping students with disabilities engaged and in school through graduation.

Due Process-A formal legal procedure under IDEA that resolves disputes between parents and schools regarding special education services.

E

Early Childhood Special Education (ECSE)-Services provided to young children (typically ages 3–5) with developmental delays or disabilities to support school readiness.

Early Intervention (EI)-Services and supports provided to infants and toddlers (birth to age 3) with developmental delays or disabilities, typically outlined in an Individualized Family Service Plan (IFSP).

Educational Advocate-An individual who assists parents and students in understanding and navigating special education processes, including IEP meetings and dispute resolution.

Educational Benefit-The progress a student is expected to make toward their IEP goals. Schools must provide an IEP reasonably calculated to enable the child to make progress appropriate in light of their circumstances (as defined by the *Endrew F.* decision).

Educational Placement-The environment in which special education services are provided to a student, such as general education classrooms, resource rooms, or specialized schools.

Emotional Disturbance (ED)-One of the 13 IDEA eligibility categories. Refers to a condition exhibiting one or more specific emotional or behavioral characteristics over a long period of time that adversely affects educational performance.

English Language Learner (ELL)-A student whose primary language is not English and who is in the process of learning English. Special education and language acquisition services may overlap but must be considered independently.

Equal Educational Opportunity-The right of every student, regardless of disability, race, language, or background, to access an education free from discrimination and barriers.

Equitable Services-Special education services that school districts must provide to eligible parentally placed private school children with disabilities, typically funded through a proportionate share of IDEA Part B funds.

Evaluation-A formal process to assess whether a student qualifies for special education services. Must be comprehensive and use a variety of assessment tools and strategies.

Extended School Year (ESY)-Special education and related services provided beyond the regular school year (e.g., summer) if the student's IEP team determines it's necessary for FAPE (Free Appropriate Public Education).

Extracurricular and Nonacademic Activities-Schools must provide students with disabilities equal opportunity to participate in activities such as clubs, sports, and afterschool programs, with necessary supports and accommodations.

F

Facilitated IEP Meeting-A type of IEP meeting led by a neutral facilitator to help the team communicate effectively and resolve disagreements, often used as an alternative dispute resolution method.

Fair Hearing-A formal legal process where parents and school districts can resolve disputes under IDEA, also known as a due process hearing.

Family Educational Rights and Privacy Act (FERPA)-A federal law that protects the privacy of student education records and gives parents the right to access and request amendments to these records.

FAPE (Free Appropriate Public Education)-A foundational principle of IDEA. It guarantees that students with disabilities are entitled to special education and related services designed to meet their unique needs at no cost to parents.

Functional Behavior Assessment (FBA)-An evaluation process used to understand the purpose or function of a student's challenging behavior, which informs the development of a Behavior Intervention Plan (BIP).

Functional Performance-Refers to how a student functions in daily activities, including social, emotional, and behavioral domains, as considered in the IEP process.

Full Inclusion-An educational philosophy that promotes educating all students, including those with significant disabilities, in the general education classroom with appropriate supports.

Frequency (of Services)-Refers to how often a service (such as speech therapy or occupational therapy) is provided, as documented in the IEP.

Friend of the Family-An informal term sometimes used to describe a support person or advocate who attends IEP meetings with a family, offering guidance and emotional support.

G

General Education-The standard curriculum presented to students without disabilities. In special education, inclusion in general education settings is a key consideration.

Generalization-The ability to apply learned skills or behaviors to new situations, environments, or people. An important goal in special education.

Gifted and Talented (GT)-Programs or services for students who demonstrate high performance capability. Some students may be twice-exceptional (gifted and have a disability).

Goals (IEP Goals)-Specific, measurable learning objectives written in a student's Individualized Education Program (IEP).

Graphic Organizer-A visual tool used to organize information, improve comprehension, and support learning for students with learning differences.

Gross Motor Skills-Abilities involving large muscle groups used for movements like walking, running, jumping, or sitting upright. Often addressed in occupational or physical therapy.

Group Therapy-A therapeutic service that may be offered in schools as part of related services under IDEA.

Guardianship-A legal process where an adult is given authority to make decisions for a person with disabilities, typically when the individual turns 18 and may not be able to make informed decisions independently.

Guidance Counselor-A school professional who supports students' academic, social, and emotional development; may be involved in the IEP process.

G-Tube (Gastrostomy Tube)-A medical device sometimes used by students with significant medical needs to receive nutrition. Requires coordination in the IEP or 504 Plan.

H

Hearing Impairment-A hearing loss that adversely affects a child's educational performance. It can range from mild to profound and may be temporary or permanent.

Health Impairment (Other Health Impairment – OHI)-A category under IDEA for students with limited strength, vitality, or alertness due to chronic or acute health problems (e.g., ADHD, diabetes, epilepsy), which adversely affect educational performance.

Homebound Instruction-Educational services provided at home or in a hospital setting for students who are unable to attend school due to medical or psychological conditions.

Homeschooling-An educational option where parents choose to educate their child at home. Children with disabilities who are homeschooled may still be entitled to certain public school services.

Home–School Communication-Strategies used to facilitate consistent and effective communication between school staff and families to support the student's IEP goals and overall success.

Hyperactivity-A condition often associated with ADHD, characterized by excessive movement, fidgeting, or difficulty remaining still or focused. It can impact a student's ability to learn in a traditional setting.

Hypersensitivity-An exaggerated response to sensory stimuli (e.g., sounds, textures, lights), common in students with autism or sensory processing disorders.

Hypotonia-Low muscle tone, often seen in students with developmental delays or neuromuscular conditions. It may affect posture, coordination, and motor skill development.

High-Functioning Autism (HFA)-A term used to describe individuals on the autism spectrum who have average to above-average intelligence and fewer language delays, though it is not an official diagnosis.

I

IDEA (Individuals with Disabilities Education Act)-A federal law ensuring services to children with disabilities throughout the nation. IDEA governs how states and public agencies provide early intervention, special education, and related services.

IEP (Individualized Education Program)-A legally binding document that outlines special education services, supports, and goals for a student with a disability. It is developed by a team that includes educators, specialists, and the child's parents or guardians.

IEP Team-The group responsible for developing, reviewing, and revising a student's IEP. It typically includes the parent(s), general and special education teachers, a school administrator, and other professionals as needed.

Inclusion-The practice of educating students with disabilities in general education classrooms alongside their peers to the maximum extent appropriate.

Independent Educational Evaluation (IEE)-An evaluation conducted by a qualified examiner not employed by the school district. Parents may request an IEE at public expense if they disagree with a school evaluation.

Individualized Family Service Plan (IFSP)
A plan for special services for young children (birth to age 3) with developmental delays. The IFSP focuses on the child and family and is often the first step in early intervention.

Informed Consent-Parental permission given with full understanding of the implications. Required before evaluations and the provision of special education services.

Instructional Accommodations-Changes in how a student accesses information or demonstrates learning without altering the curriculum. Examples include extra time on tests or preferred seating.

Intellectual Disability-A disability characterized by significant limitations in both intellectual functioning and adaptive behavior. It is one of the 13 eligibility categories under IDEA.

Intervention-Targeted strategies or programs used to address specific academic or behavioral needs before or in addition to special education services.

J

Job Coach-A professional who supports students with disabilities in workplace settings. They provide on-the-job training, help develop job skills, and support independence.

Job Shadowing-A career exploration activity where a student observes a professional in a real-world job setting. Often part of transition planning for students with IEPs.

Joint Attention-A foundational social-communication skill where two individuals focus on the same object or event. Difficulties with joint attention are often seen in children with autism.

Juvenile Detention Center Education-Educational programs provided to youth with disabilities who are placed in secure facilities. These programs must meet federal requirements under IDEA.

Juvenile Justice System-A legal system for individuals under 18 who are accused of committing a crime. Students with disabilities involved in this system still have rights to receive educational services under IDEA and Section 504.

K

Key Terms – Often used in special education glossaries or legal documents to identify crucial concepts.

Kindergarten Readiness – Refers to the skills and behaviors children need to succeed in kindergarten, including social-emotional and developmental benchmarks, which are important for early identification and intervention.

Kinesthetic Learning – A learning style in which students learn best through physical activities and hands-on experiences; often considered when developing an Individualized Education Program (IEP) for students with specific learning preferences.

Knowledge-Based Learning – Instruction focused on building a student's background knowledge, which can be particularly important for students with language-based learning disabilities.

KTEA (Kaufman Test of Educational Achievement) – A standardized test used by school psychologists to assess academic skills in areas like reading, math, and written language, commonly used during special education evaluations.

L

Language-Based Learning Disability (LBLD) – A type of learning disability affecting skills such as listening, speaking, reading, writing, and spelling, often addressed through speech-language therapy and specialized instruction.

Language Disorder – A communication disorder that affects a student's ability to understand or use spoken, written, or other language systems, often impacting educational performance.

Learning Disability (LD) – A neurological disorder that affects the brain's ability to receive, process, store, or respond to information, commonly addressed in special education plans.

Least Restrictive Environment (LRE) – A fundamental principle under IDEA requiring that students with disabilities be educated with their non-disabled peers to the greatest extent appropriate.

Letter of Understanding – A written document that clarifies what was discussed or agreed upon during an IEP meeting or other school communication, though not a legally binding contract.

Local Education Agency (LEA) – Typically the public school district responsible for ensuring that students receive special education services under IDEA.

Low Incidence Disability – A disability that occurs relatively infrequently (e.g., blindness, deafness, severe intellectual disabilities), requiring specialized educational strategies and support.

M

Mainstreaming – The practice of placing students with disabilities in general education classrooms for part or all of the school day, often seen as a step toward inclusion.

Manifestation Determination Review (MDR) – A meeting required under IDEA to determine if a student's behavior that led to disciplinary action was caused by or had a direct relationship to their disability.

MAP (Measure of Academic Progress) – A standardized assessment often used to track a student's academic growth over time, which may be part of a special education evaluation or progress monitoring.

Mediation – A voluntary process facilitated by a neutral third party to resolve disputes between parents and schools regarding special education services.

Medical Services (for diagnostic or evaluation purposes) – Under IDEA, these are services provided by a licensed physician to determine a child's medically related disability that results in the child's need for special education and related services.

Mentor Teacher – An experienced educator who supports and guides special education teachers or paraprofessionals, especially those new to the field.

Mobility Impairment – A physical disability that limits a student's ability to move independently, often requiring accommodations such as accessible classrooms or assistive devices.

Modifications – Changes to what a student is expected to learn. Unlike accommodations (which change how they learn), modifications alter the curriculum or performance expectations.

Multidisciplinary Team (MDT) – A group of professionals (e.g., teachers, psychologists, therapists) who collaborate to evaluate and develop services for a student with a disability.

Multiple Disabilities – A special education eligibility category under IDEA where a student has two or more disabling conditions that significantly impact educational performance and require special education services.

N

Native Language – The language normally used by an individual or their parents; IDEA requires evaluations and communication to be provided in the parent's native language whenever possible.

NCLB (No Child Left Behind) – Although now replaced by ESSA (Every Student Succeeds Act), NCLB was a major federal education law that emphasized accountability and progress for all students, including those in special education.

Needs-Based Services – Services provided based on the individual needs of the student, rather than their category of disability or placement.

Nonverbal Learning Disability (NVLD) – A neurological disorder characterized by difficulties with visual-spatial, motor, and social skills, despite strong verbal abilities.

Notice of Procedural Safeguards – A document that outlines the legal rights of parents and students under IDEA; schools must provide this at least once a year and under specific circumstances.

Noncompliance – When a student fails to follow directions or rules, often considered during behavior assessments; can also refer to a school's failure to follow IEP requirements.

Norm-Referenced Test – A type of standardized test that compares a student's performance to that of a norm group; often used during special education evaluations.

Neurological Disorder – A disorder that affects the nervous system and can impact learning, attention, communication, or physical functioning (e.g., epilepsy, Tourette syndrome, ADHD).

Nonpublic School Placement – When a district places a student with a disability in a private (nonpublic) school because the public school cannot meet their needs, under IDEA provisions.

O

Objective – A measurable, short-term goal written as part of an IEP to help guide instruction and track progress toward broader annual goals.

Occupational Therapy (OT) – A related service under IDEA that helps students with disabilities develop, recover, or maintain skills needed for daily living and academic tasks (e.g., handwriting, fine motor skills, self-care).

Office for Civil Rights (OCR) – A federal agency within the U.S. Department of Education that enforces civil rights laws (in theory only in my opinion), including those protecting students with disabilities from discrimination.

Office for Civil Rights (OCR) – A federal agency within the U.S. Department of Justice that enforces civil rights laws, including those protecting students with disabilities from discrimination.

One-to-One Aide – An individual assigned to support a student with significant needs throughout the school day; can assist with academics, behavior, mobility, or personal care.

Orientation and Mobility (O&M) – Services provided to students who are blind or visually impaired to help them safely and independently navigate their environments.

Other Health Impairment (OHI) – An IDEA eligibility category for students with limited strength, vitality, or alertness due to chronic or acute health problems (e.g., ADHD, epilepsy, diabetes) that adversely affect educational performance.

Out-of-District Placement – When a student is placed in a school outside their local district because the educational needs cannot be met within their local district.

P

Paraprofessional – A school staff member who supports students with disabilities under the supervision of a certified teacher, often providing academic or behavioral assistance.

Parent Training and Information Center (PTI) – Federally funded centers that provide parents with information, training, and support related to special education and disability rights.

Physical Therapy (PT) – A related service under IDEA focused on improving a student's gross motor skills, mobility, and physical functioning necessary for school participation.

Placement – The educational environment in which a student with a disability receives special education services; must be based on the IEP and support the Least Restrictive Environment (LRE) principle.

Positive Behavioral Interventions and Supports (PBIS) – A proactive approach to improving school climate and reducing problem behaviors through evidence-based strategies and systems.

Present Levels of Academic Achievement and Functional Performance (PLAAFP) – A section of the IEP that describes a student's current abilities and how their disability affects participation and progress in the general curriculum.

Prior Written Notice (PWN) – A legal requirement under IDEA that schools must give written notice
to parents before proposing or refusing to initiate or change the identification, evaluation, or placement of a student.

Private Evaluation – An assessment conducted by a professional outside the school system, which parents may request or obtain independently to support their concerns or requests for services.

Procedural Safeguards – Legal protections under IDEA that ensure parents and students are informed of their rights regarding special education decisions and dispute resolution.

Progress Monitoring – The regular and systematic assessment of a student's academic or behavioral performance to determine the effectiveness of instruction or intervention.

Q

Qualified Personnel – Under IDEA, individuals who meet the necessary qualifications, certifications, and experience to provide special education services to students with disabilities (e.g., teachers, therapists, specialists).

Quality Indicators – Standards used to measure the effectiveness of special education programs, services, and supports, ensuring that students with disabilities receive appropriate and high-quality education.

Quantitative Data – Objective, numerical data used to measure a student's progress, often included in special education assessments or evaluations to track performance over time.

Questionnaire – A tool often used in assessments or evaluations to gather information from parents, teachers, or students themselves about the student's needs, strengths, and areas of concern.

Quick-Start IEP – A simplified version of an Individualized Education Program (IEP) that may be developed as a temporary plan while more comprehensive assessments and decisions are being made.

R

Reading Disability – A type of learning disability that affects a student's ability to read, often characterized by difficulties with decoding, fluency, or comprehension.

Reevaluation – The process of assessing a student with a disability periodically to determine whether their educational needs have changed and to review the adequacy of the current IEP. A reevaluation must occur at least every three years under IDEA, but can be done more frequently if necessary.

Referral – The formal process of requesting an evaluation for special education services. This can be initiated by a parent, teacher, or other professional when there are concerns about a child's learning or behavior.

Rehabilitation Act of 1973, Section 504 – A federal law that prohibits discrimination based on disability in programs and activities, including education. Section 504 ensures that students with disabilities receive accommodations to participate in school activities and programs.

Reinforcement – A strategy used in behavior management, where a behavior is encouraged by providing a reward (positive reinforcement) or removing a negative stimulus (negative reinforcement). Reinforcement is often used in special education to promote desired behaviors.

Related Services – Services provided to students with disabilities that are necessary for them to benefit from special education. This may include services like speech therapy, occupational therapy, physical therapy, counseling, and transportation.

Resolution Session – A meeting required under IDEA when parents file a complaint or request a due process hearing. The resolution session provides an opportunity for the school and parents to resolve disputes before proceeding to a formal hearing.

Resource Room – A separate classroom where students with disabilities receive specialized instruction and support in areas such as reading, math, or behavior. Students spend part of their day in the resource room and the rest in a general education setting, depending on their needs.

Response to Intervention (RTI) – A multi-tiered approach to identifying and supporting students with learning and behavior needs. RTI involves providing interventions at increasing levels of intensity to determine whether a student's difficulties can be resolved with support before considering a special education evaluation.

Rights of Parents and Students – Under IDEA, parents and students have specific legal rights regarding their participation in special education processes, including the right to be informed, to consent, and to appeal decisions. These rights ensure that families can advocate for their child's needs.

S

Section 504 – Part of the Rehabilitation Act of 1973 that prohibits discrimination based on disability in any program or activity receiving federal financial assistance, including schools. Students who qualify for Section 504 receive accommodations to ensure equal access to education.

Self-Advocacy – The ability of students to understand and communicate their own needs and preferences, often supported through training and skill-building to ensure they can actively participate in their educational planning.

Significant Cognitive Disability (SCD) – A term used to describe students who have substantial limitations in intellectual functioning and adaptive behavior, which affects their ability to participate in general education without significant modifications.

Social-Emotional Learning (SEL) – The process of developing the skills to understand and manage emotions, set and achieve positive goals, show empathy for others, maintain positive relationships, and make responsible decisions.

Special Education – Tailored instruction designed to meet the unique needs of students with disabilities, ensuring they have access to a free and appropriate public education (FAPE) under IDEA.

Special Education Teacher – An educator trained to work with students who have a variety of disabilities, providing individualized instruction and support in a range of settings.

Speech and Language Therapy – A related service under IDEA that addresses communication disorders, including speech delays, language impairments, and difficulties with social communication.

Student-Directed IEP – An IEP process where the student takes a central role in discussing their strengths, needs, and goals, promoting independence and self-advocacy in their educational journey.

Supplementary Aids and Services – Supports and services provided in general education settings to help students with disabilities participate in the same activities as their peers, including assistive technology, modified materials, and classroom aides.

Suspension – A disciplinary action where a student is temporarily removed from school for violating behavior policies. For students with disabilities, a manifestation determination must be made to assess if the behavior is related to the student's disability.

T

Teacher of the Deaf or Hard of Hearing (TDHH) – An educator who works with students who have hearing impairments, providing specialized instruction and support to help them succeed in both general and special education settings.

Teacher of the Visually Impaired (TVI) – A specialized educator who works with students who have visual impairments, helping them develop skills and strategies to access education effectively.

Temporary Placement – A short-term educational setting or service placement for a student, often used during a transition period, while awaiting a more permanent solution based on the student's needs.

Test Accommodation – Modifications made to testing procedures for students with disabilities to ensure equal access to assessment, such as extended time, alternative formats, or a quiet environment.

Therapeutic Day School – A type of school that provides specialized services for students with emotional or behavioral disabilities, often with a focus on mental health services in addition to academics.

Tiers of Intervention – The levels of support provided in a Response to Intervention (RTI) system. Tiers range from universal interventions for all students to intensive, individualized support for those who are struggling the most.

Total Communication – An approach used with students who are deaf or hard of hearing, combining sign language, spoken language, gestures, and other communication methods to meet the student's needs.

Transition Plan – Part of the IEP that outlines the goals and services needed to support a student's transition from school to adulthood, including education, vocational training, and independent living skills.

Transition Services – Services designed to help students with disabilities move from school to post-school activities, such as higher education, employment, and independent living. Transition planning must begin by the time the student turns 16 (or earlier, depending on state laws).

Traumatic Brain Injury (TBI) – An acquired injury to the brain caused by an external physical force, often resulting in physical, cognitive, or emotional impairments that can affect a student's ability to participate in school.

U

Underachievement – When a student performs below their expected level, often due to factors such as a disability, lack of appropriate support, or insufficient intervention.

Understanding by Design (UbD) – An approach to curriculum design that emphasizes backward planning, where educators first define the desired learning outcomes and then design instruction to achieve those outcomes.

Unilateral Placement – When parents place their child in a private school or another setting without the agreement of the public school district, often due to dissatisfaction with the services provided under the student's IEP.

Unique Needs – The specific and individualized educational needs of students with disabilities, which are considered when developing an Individualized Education Program (IEP) to ensure they receive an appropriate education.

Universal Design for Learning (UDL) – An educational framework that aims to make learning accessible to all students by providing multiple means of representation, expression, and engagement to address diverse learning styles and abilities.

Universal Screening – The process of assessing all students in a given population to identify those who may be at risk for learning difficulties or disabilities, often used as part of a Response to Intervention (RTI) process.

Urgent Needs – Critical, immediate educational or support needs identified for students with disabilities that must be addressed to ensure they can participate in their education effectively.

V

Valid Evaluation – An assessment or evaluation process that accurately measures a student's abilities, needs, and disabilities to inform decisions about special education services and placement.

Verbal Behavior – A teaching approach based on the principles of Applied Behavior Analysis (ABA) that focuses on developing communication skills through verbal interactions. It is often used for students with autism or communication disorders.

Vested Rights – Legal rights that are guaranteed to students, such as the right to an appropriate education, the right to a free and appropriate public education (FAPE), and the right to access special education services under IDEA.

Vision Support Services – Specialized services provided to students with visual impairments, including the use of assistive technology, braille instruction, or vision therapy to support learning and participation in school activities.

Visual Impairment – A disability that affects a student's ability to see, which may be due to blindness or other conditions such as low vision. Students with visual impairments may require specialized instruction and accommodations to access education.

Vocational Education – Instruction and training provided to students to prepare them for specific careers or trades. It includes skills and knowledge necessary for employment in fields such as technology, healthcare, and the arts.

Vocational Rehabilitation – Services designed to help students with disabilities transition to the workforce, including job training, placement, and support to help them gain and maintain employment.

W

Wheelchair Accessibility – The design and modification of school facilities and classrooms to ensure that students who use wheelchairs can access and participate in school activities and navigate the school environment safely.

Whole-Child Approach – An educational philosophy that focuses on addressing the full spectrum of a student's needs, including cognitive, social, emotional, physical, and behavioral needs, in order to support their overall development and well-being.

Withdrawal – A term used to describe the removal of a student from a particular class, program, or setting, either temporarily or permanently, for reasons such as behavioral concerns or medical needs.

Workplace Readiness – Skills and behaviors that are necessary for success in the workplace, including communication, teamwork, problem-solving, and time management. Vocational training programs often focus on helping students develop workplace readiness.

Wraparound Services – A comprehensive, individualized approach to support students with disabilities, addressing their academic, behavioral, emotional, and social needs through a coordinated network of services and support.

Wrightslaw – A well-known resource for parents, educators, and advocates in the field of special education law. It provides information on educational rights, IDEA, and strategies for advocating for children with disabilities.

Written Expression – The ability to communicate effectively through writing. Students with disabilities may receive specialized instruction and accommodations to improve their written communication skills.

X

Xerophthalmia – A medical condition that affects the eyes, leading to dryness, irritation, and potential blindness if untreated. It may require special education accommodations for students with visual impairments.

X-linked Disorder – A genetic disorder linked to the X chromosome, which can lead to developmental disabilities or other conditions. These disorders may affect males more severely due to having only one X chromosome.

Y

Yardstick Measurement – A term sometimes used in educational contexts to refer to a standard or benchmark used to measure a student's progress or achievement, particularly in assessing educational outcomes for students with disabilities.

Young Children with Disabilities – Refers to children aged 3 to 5 who have disabilities and are eligible for special education services under IDEA. These children may receive early intervention services designed to support their development in areas such as speech, motor skills, and social-emotional growth.

Z

Zero Reject Principle – A core concept in special education under IDEA (Individuals with Disabilities Education Act), which mandates that no student with a disability can be excluded from receiving a free and appropriate public education (FAPE). Schools must provide services to all students with disabilities, regardless of the severity of their condition.

A

Academic	10, 18, 30, 31, 45, 51-52, 57-58, 66-67, 70
Access	9-10, 13, 18-19, 28-29, 32, 34-35, 38-40, 44, 50-51, 56-57, 59-61, 70, 21
Accommodation	18, 30, 50-52, 61, 72
Accredit	60
Achieve	30-31, 43, 48, 50, 57, 75, 77
Administra	9, 15-16, 27, 57, 63
Advoca	2, 6, 12, 44
Aid	26, 75
Align	19
Alternat	36, 40, 55, 57-58, 62, 65-66, 70
Annual	34, 57, 59
Assess	28, 31, 33, 40, 42, 48-49, 59, 68
Assist	9, 20, 26, 31, 48-49, 57, 61
Asynchronous	60
Attend	9-10, 54-57, 60, 70, 74, 83, 86-87
Autism	67

B

Basic	59
Behavior	8, 10, 15, 19, 30-31, 37, 42-43, 48, 51, 57, 64-66, 69, 70
Bench	58
Board	11, 15-16, 31, 38, 44-45, 48, 54, 58, 65, 77-78
Bully	9-10, 18

C

Child Find	12
Case Manager	9, 13, 16, 18-19, 22, 25, 33, 36-39, 53, 65, 73
Curriculum	57-60
Classroom	15, 30, 41, 45, 53, 60, 67, 74-75
Consent	26, 28, 31, 34-35, 42, 46-48, 64, 66, 71, 82
Collaborative	36-37, 70
Compensatory	12
Counsel	9, 30
Correct	9-12, 15, 19, 28-29, 68
Communication	37, 64
Close	30, 57
Check	16, 47, 53, 55

D

Data	39, 66
Deaf	19
Designate	53, 57
Developmental	E30
Disability	1-2, 8-10, 18, 21, 31-32, 49-51, 61-62, 64, 67, 72
Disproportion	51, 73
Different	12, 20, 22, 46, 52-53, 64
Direct	11, 21, 41, 43, 63, 70
Due	6, 11-14, 32, 35-37, 48, 61, 62, 65, 68, 70

E

Early	30, 51, 65, 77
Educational	2, 12-14, 18-19, 28-31, 36-37, 41, 44, 47-49, 52, 55-63, 65-66, 69-70-71, 77
Emotional	10, 29, 30, 31, 48, 51
Equal	10, 17-18, 25, 32, 41, 50, 72
Evaluation	13-14, 30-31, 37, 48-49, 51, 66-67
Extend	9, 61
Extra	19, 32, 59

F

Facilitate	36-37
Fair	18, 32, 36
Family	28-29, 41, 43, 56, 59, 67
FAPE	12-14, 35, 49, 68-70
Function	31, 42, 48, 58
Full	10, 34, 41-42, 48, 50, 60-61, 70, 72, 75
Frequency	45

G

Goal	36, 43, 56, 70
Group	10, 12, 18, 44
12-Guardianship	8, 10-12, 29, 31, 33, 35, 41-42, 45, 47-50, 54, 57, 59, 61, 63, 66-72, 74
Guidance	1

H

Hear	12-14, 16, 25, 31-32, 36-37, 48, 63, 65, 67-68
Health	30-31, 34-35, 44
Homeschool	59
High	19, 53, 55, 57, 60, 78

www.ingramcontent.com/pod-product-compliance
Lightning Source LLC
Chambersburg PA
CBHW050926150426
42812CB00051B/2435